New State Formations in Education Policy

EDUCATIONAL FUTURES
RETHINKING THEORY AND PRACTICE
Volume 39

Series Editors
Michael A. Peters
University of Illinois at Urbana-Champaign, USA

Editorial Board

Michael Apple, *University of Wisconsin-Madison, USA*
Miriam David, *Institute of Education, London University, UK*
Cushla Kapitzke, *Queensland University of Technology, Australia*
Simon Marginson, *University of Melbourne, Australia*
Mark Olssen, *University of Surrey, UK*
Fazal Rizvi, *University of Illinois at Urbana-Champaign, USA*
Linda Tuahwai Smith, *University of Waikato, New Zealand*
Susan Robertson, *University of Bristol, UK*

Scope
This series maps the emergent field of educational futures. It will commission books on the futures of education in relation to the question of globalisation and knowledge economy. It seeks authors who can demonstrate their understanding of discourses of the knowledge and learning economies. It aspires to build a consistent approach to educational futures in terms of traditional methods, including scenario planning and foresight, as well as imaginative narratives, and it will examine examples of futures research in education, pedagogical experiments, new utopian thinking, and educational policy futures with a strong accent on actual policies and examples.

New State Formations in Education Policy

Reflections from Spain

Laura C. Engel
The George Washington University, USA

SENSE PUBLISHERS
ROTTERDAM/BOSTON/TAIPEI

A C.I.P. record for this book is available from the Library of Congress.

ISBN 978-94-6091-063-0 (paperback)
ISBN 978-94-6091-064-7 (hardback)
ISBN 978-94-6091-065-4 (e-book)

Published by: Sense Publishers,
P.O. Box 21858, 3001 AW
Rotterdam, The Netherlands
http://www.sensepublishers.com

Printed on acid-free paper

Cover by Michael Scheffki

To Matt Youngblood

TABLE OF CONTENTS

PREFACE

This book is based on research conducted in 2003-2007 as part of a PhD thesis. My interest in taking on this project, and in this book, is to understand how, in an era of globalization, education policy has been produced in the post-Franco period in Spain, with respect both to regional pressures from Catalonia for greater autonomy and pressures for greater European integration. The central aim is to provide perspectives on a number of the processes surrounding education policy formation through an exploration of educational decentralization in Catalonia and Spain. Although the formal project began in 2003, my interest in Spain and its educational reform processes began much earlier, in both my formal studies of Spanish language, history and literature, and my encounters and numerous stays in Sevilla, Madrid and Barcelona over the past decade. It has been these experiences in both Catalonia and Spain which served to initiate my interest in nation state (re)formations and education policy production.

What emerges through this book is a perspective of modern day Spain, in which policy-makers in Catalonia have to take into account and negotiate not only local traditions and issues but also policy ideas emanating from the national government in Madrid, the developing European agenda, and notions circulating within the global space. In this way, policy concepts surrounding educational decentralization are not only formed in relation to national-regional dynamics but are influenced more broadly by a more complex set of supranational and global considerations. Moving beyond state-centrism, this study illustrates that policy is no longer produced in a self-contained and hermetically sealed space, national or local, but is influenced by inputs arising from a range of different sources. Moreover, this study illustrates in education policy terms, how endogenous and exogenous processes intersect in a number of complicated ways.

Ultimately, post-Franco Spain offers a dynamic story that exemplifies globalization's hand in the modern nation state's process of continuous reconstruction and rebirth. The vibrant issues present in the case of Catalonia, Spain and Europe echo the challenges and complexities facing nation state apparatuses in the divisive and malleable 21st century globalized world. The complexity of these issues seems to have particular resonance with the political and economic environment that we live in today, marked very recently by the global economic crisis. In the wake of financial shockwaves felt around the world, following the fall of Lehman Brothers in September 2008, perspectives on globalization and the ways in which modern states perceive and manage the demands of a new global economy have never been more important.

The global economic crisis, which has become equally disruptive to states, regions and supranational organizations worldwide, has increased the significance of key questions about the organization of states and governance structures, as well as pressures informing education policy. For example, how will devolved states, like Spain, situate themselves within the global political and economic playing field, and how will governance, including in education, be influenced? In what ways will an expanding supranational entity, like the European Union, be affected and how will it respond to the financial crisis? What role will regions (continue to) play in the articulation and the enactment of the EU's economic and political imperatives? These questions point to the fact that more so than ever, studies of political, economic and cultural globalization and new state formations in education, are important for understanding current governance structures and education policy-making processes.

LCE
Nottingham, United Kingdom
May 2009

ACKNOWLEDGMENTS

In taking on this project, I am indebted to many individuals and institutions. The ideas for this book have their roots at the University of Illinois, where I benefited from the inspiring ideas and the valuable critical feedback from many different individuals, particularly David Rutkowski, Jason Sparks, Leslie Rutkowski, Nicole Lamers, Michael Peters, Nicholas Burbules, Jan Nederveen Pieterse, Bob Pahre, Eun Young Kim, and Zsuzsa Gille. I would like to especially thank Fazal Rizvi, who for over the past five years, has offered his encouragement, guidance, and expertise, all of which I am deeply grateful. I would also like to thank Cameron McCarthy, both for his generous support of this work and for including me in the Friday research and publication collaborative at the University of Illinois. I owe thanks to Susan Robertson and Roger Dale for helping me to further develop these ideas during a Worldwide Universities Network research studentship at University of Bristol. I am also grateful to Debora Hinderliter Ortloff, who has recently helped me to see the case of Catalonia and Spain in a comparative light, and therefore offered valuable insights into this work. While at the University of Nottingham, I benefited greatly from working with colleagues at the UNESCO Centre for Comparative Educational Research, and especially with John Holford and the many "European partners" linked to the Includ-ED and Lifelong Learning 2010 projects. Thank you also to Michael Peters, Peter de Liefde, Bernice Kelly, and Sense Publishers for their technical assistance in the preparation of this manuscript.

This project was supported by a number of different fellowships and studentships. First is the European Union Center at the University of Illinois, which provided support through its Foreign Language and Area Studies annual and summer grants. These fellowships allowed me to spend extensive time immersed in the study of Catalan, Castilian Spanish and EU Area Studies, as well as helped to support my fieldwork research in Europe. Thanks are also due to the Bureau of Educational Research at the College of Education at the University of Illinois for the dissertation grant. Lastly, I would like to recognize the financial support provided by the Graduate College at the University of Illinois through the Dissertation Completion Award.

As this book is based upon fieldwork research conducted across three different sites: Barcelona, Madrid and Brussels, I would like to thank the policy-makers, government officials, and the individuals from educational agencies and organizations, who agreed to be interviewed for this study. I would also like to thank the *Institut d' Estudis Catalans* (Institute of Catalan Studies) in Barcelona, for providing me with access to their collections of reports and other published materials. Thank you to Xavier Bonal, Aina Tarabini-Castellani Clemente and other colleagues at the Autonomous University of Barcelona for your help and to Aina for generously giving me a home in Barcelona. Thanks also to Peter Jones for facilitating interviews at the European Commission, and for generally enriching the time that I spent in Brussels.

ACKNOWLEDGMENTS

I have learned a lot in the process of working on this project. However, it would not have been nearly as enjoyable without the support and good company of friends and family. I am especially indebted to my parents, John and Karen Engel, to Tom and Dorothy Youngblood, and to my sister Beth Engel. Finally I would like to thank my husband and greatest friend of all, Matt Youngblood. I dedicate this book to Matt, who has a presence in every aspect of this work and in each page of this book.

LIST OF ABBREVIATIONS AND ACRONYMS

AJEC	Association of Young Students of Catalonia
APSEC	Professional Association of Education Services of Catalonia
CCAA	Autonomous Communities
CC.OO	Comisiones Obreras - Workers' Commissions
CDC	Convergencia Democrática de Catalunya
CiU	Convergéncia I Unió - Convergence and Union
COR	Committee of the Regions
EC	European Community
ECSC	European Coal and Steel Community
EEC	European Economic Community
ERC	Republican Left of Catalonia
EU	European Union
FAPAC	Federation of Associations of Parents and Students
FAPAES	Federation of Parents' Associations of Secondary Schools of Catalonia
FAPEL	Federation of Parents' Associations of Free (Independents) Schools' of Catalonia
FCI	Inter-Territorial Compensation Fund
FET	Falange Española Tradicionalista y de las Juntas de Ofensive Nacional-Sindicalista
GDP	Gross Domestic Product
GNP	Gross National Product
ICV-EUiA	Green Initiative for Catalonia-United and Alternative Left
IOs	International Organizations
LOAPA	Organic Law for the Harmonization of the Process of Self-Government
LOCE	Organic Law on Quality in Education
LODE	Regulatory Organic Law of the Right to Education
LOE	Organic Law of Education
LOECE	Organic Law of the Statute of Scholastic Centers
LOGSE	Organic Law on the General Organization of the Educational System
LOPEG	Organic Law on Participation, Assessment and Governance of Institutions of Education
MEC	Ministerio de Educación y Ciencia - Ministry of Education and Science
MEPSYD	Ministerio de Educación, Política Social y Deporte - Ministry of Education, Social Policy and Sport
NATO	North Atlantic Trade Organization
NPM	New Public Management
NGO	Nongovernmental Organization
OECD	Organization of Economic and Co-operative Development

LIST OF ABBREVIATIONS AND ACRONYMS

OMC	Open Method of Coordination
PISA	Programme for International Student Assessment
PP	Partido Popular - Popular Party
PSC	Socialist Party of Catalonia
PSOE	Partido Socialista Obrero Español - Spanish Socialist Workers' Party
UCD	Unión de Centro Democrático - Democratic Center Union
UDC	Unió Democràtica de Catalunya - Part of the CiU
UGT	Unión General de Trabajadores - General Workers' Union
UN	United Nations
UNESCO	United Nations Educational, Scientific and Cultural Organization
USOC	Worker's Union of Catalonia
USTEC	Union of Teaching Workers of Catalonia

CHAPTER 1

NEW STATE FORMATIONS IN EDUCATION POLICY

Education has long been a tool for the construction of the modern nation state system, through the building of core institutions and infrastructure and the binding of citizens under an assembled and forged sense of common national identity (Green, 1997). As a result of global economic competition, an increasingly crowded policy stage of new (supranational and regional) actors, and the realities and tensions surrounding the increased mobility, collision and displacement of people, modern states have been influenced by a range of political, economic and cultural forces. As a result, the nation state itself is being reconfigured by global and supranational actors "from above," regional and local actors "from below," and new challenges of immigration (Telò, 2002). These dynamic shifts are sparking new developments in education policy and reconfiguring new modes of governance in education. Thus, education is a lens through which to better understand the dynamic and complex shifts of the nation state in the generation of and response to global forces.

While the development of education policy agendas seems to remain under the authority of national governments, governments are rewriting policies to align with global and supranational imperatives (Burbules & Torres, 2000; Dale & Robertson, 2002), the development and impact of new policy spaces in education (cf. Nóvoa & Lawn, 2002) and the realities of new migration patterns of people across borders. As the state negotiates these global and supranational pressures "from above," new modes of education governance are being produced, which place greater importance on local and regional scales in terms of the direction of policy development. Indeed, the role of the nation state in education appears to have shifted, particularly as national education systems around the world face significant global and supranational pressures on the development of education policy, and seek to reconcile these with local and regional traditions and priorities.

Against this backdrop, *New State Formations in Education Policy: Reflections from Spain* is an intervention in the study of globalization and education. This book seeks to focus on how global processes have led to new state formations, linked to the opening up of new spaces both above and below the nation state, raising significant questions about education and education policy in the 21st century. In *New State Formations*, I draw on the case of modern day Spain, which is both interesting and instructive in framing shifts in education policy, regionalization and Europeanization processes. The book develops its arguments around a focus of the numerous and complex pressures facing the modern Spanish education system stem from simultaneous efforts in the post-Franco era of democratization, decentralization, globalization, and Europeanization, with Spain's 1986 accession into what was at the time the European Community (EC). The nature and scope of these efforts and their influence on Spanish public institutions, including education, appear to be driven by policy pressures emanating from supranational (EU) and global processes, as well as local, regional, and national politics.

Consequently, education policy, particularly in relation to governance, is being produced in response to complex aims and agendas stemming from a wide range of political, economic, social, and cultural interests. These issues encountered in the case of Spain and new Europe reverberate the challenges and complexities facing state apparatuses in the 21st century, globalized world. States, which after all are made up of human actors, are ultimately forced to reconcile contradictory pressures of a malleable and divisive world in which we live. Thus, while the story told here is grounded in post-Franco Spain in relation to regionalism and European integration, it is a dynamic case that exemplifies globalization's hand in the modern nation state's process of continuous formation and reformation.

EDUCATION POLICY FORMATION PROCESSES

From context, negotiation and production to implementation, evaluation and alternatives, education policy involves a spectrum of distinct stages. In the initial stages of policy are the policy context, policy influences and pressures, policy negotiation, and the production of policy. The primary interest of this book is in these front-end stages of policy influences (pressures), policy negotiation, and policy development. First, to understand, implement, evaluate, and offer alternatives to education policy, researchers need to enquire about the nature of pressures and the processes of policy negotiation and production. This allows for an understanding of how the political pressures influence the content of a particular policy, as well as provide an understanding of the outcomes and the alternatives that exist. Second, the primary stages of policy pinpointed bring agency to the forefront of policy negotiation and production. Against the grain of more structuralist analyses, this study views the state as "breathed into being" by actors exercising their agency in various ways, in reaction to numerous pressures.

Writing about the multiple stages of policy, Easton's (1965) system theory distinguished environmental inputs (demands and support) in political systems that are translated through processes of negotiation into outputs (decisions and actions). These outputs then cycle back, as they are debated, implemented, evaluated, and adjusted. What Easton (1965) framed as inputs and negotiation within the political system, in this case, align with the initial stages of policy outlined above. The latter stages of implementation, outcomes, evaluation, and suggested alternatives represent Easton's output stage. Many criticisms have been made of Easton's political system as an overly neat, simplified, and rational ordering of how decisions become made (Ham & Hill, 1993).

While helpful in viewing multiple stages of policy and policy analysis, Easton's framework raises a concern about the portrayal of "policy [a]s assembled in stages, as if on a conveyer belt" (Stone, 2002, p. xii). As pointed out by Ham and Hill (1993), these approaches to policy analysis tend to overlook government action by placing it in a "black box" labeled the political system (p. 16). Nonetheless, drawing distinctions between multiple stages of policy are helpful for framing the perspective of the approach to policy and policy analysis embodied in this study. The perspective on education policy taken up in this book stands against rational or instrumental approaches, which have dominated approaches to studies of education and education policy analysis, beginning in the 1960s with the work of Easton (1965) and Dror (1968). Rationalist approaches to policy studies and policy analysis often assume an objective stance on policy, and tend to focus on the ways in which the assumed rational individual, induced by her/his own concerns, acts in relation to institutional rules and regulations (Sabatier, 1999).

In contrast to rationalist approaches, this book begins the assumption that there cannot be an understanding of policy unless it is located within a larger political, economic, social, and cultural context. Stone (1988) argued, "both policy and thinking about policy are produced in political communities" (p. 7). This means that the construction, negotiation, and implementation of policy are at times inflicted with contrasting values, ideas, and ideologies. Moreover, education policy formation processes as uneven, contentious, and widely debated. In this framework for examining education policy, policy is not viewed as static or objective. Rather, policy is considered to be produced in a particular economic, political, cultural, and social context, with contrasting political interests reflected in the production of particular policies.

In Ball's (1994) work, policy is both text and discourse. Policy as discourse, he argued, reaches beyond the analysis of policy text to critically address the production of policy discourse. This approach reaches beyond the analysis of text to also include questions regarding the spaces in which discourses originate, the major agents that produce discourse, and the ways in which discourses are reflected in individual usage. This has particular implications for education policy research, in which an analysis of documents is not only concerned with what is included in the actual policy text, but also the processes of policy negotiation and construction, as well as the larger context in which the policies are produced.

In order to capture the processes and politics of policy negotiation and production, the approach or perspective to policy within this book does not see policy as separate from context, but rather the context is the terrain from which policy problems are developed and understood (Ozga, 2000). In this investigation, the complexities of the policy production process are at the center of my approach to policy analysis. As Ball (1990) argued, the field of policy analysis is flush with

> abstract accounts [which] tend towards tidy generalities and often fail to capture the messy realities of influence, pressure, dogma, expediency, conflict, compromise, intransigence, resistance, error, opposition and pragmatism in the policy process. It is easy to be simple, neat and superficial and to gloss over these awkward realities. It is difficult to retain messiness and complexity and still be penetrating. (p. 9)

My emphasis throughout this book is to engage the messiness of education policy production processes in a way that highlights the agency of individual system actors involved in the overlap of local, regional, national, and supranational spheres. In theorizing the production of policy across local, regional, national, supranational (EU), and global political spheres, larger policy processes must be analyzed, including various actors, conflicting tensions, and contextual factors. In this way, we can understand the ways in which education policy is constructed in relation to multiscalar pressures, and a conceptual understanding of the human agents, their perceptions and experiences in policy-making. In viewing policy in this way, education policy, like no other area of social policy, can offer a unique lens on globalization, regionalization and shifts in the nation state.

BEYOND BINARY OPPOSITIONS

Contemporary debates about globalization, nation state reformation, and education policy production have tended to highlight global pressures from the top down, demonstrating the complex ways that global forces and pressures are reshaping national systems of education. This places the sole emphasis on the nature of the relationship between the global and the nation-state, which Dale (2005) has critiqued as a zero-sum game: where one wins, the other loses. Yet, much of the literature of education policy in Europe and the Europeanization of education have pursued similar lines in their focus on the impact of developing European education priorities on national education systems, thus framing the study around the state as a fixed entity.

These dominant global-nation state or Europe-nation state frameworks overlook the nature of the relationship that new regional actors have with both the nation-state and supranational (EU) actors. The tendencies to rely on nation state-global and nation state-Europe constructs appear to remain dependant on "spatial fetishism" and "methodological nationalism" (Brenner, 2004). This refers to the presupposition of the exclusivity and the static territorial, political, and economic stronghold of the nation state in policy production. Methodological nationalism, as first discussed by Martins (1974), is "the assumption that the nation/state/society is the natural social and political form of the modern world" (Wimmer & Schiller, 2002, p. 302). The reliance on such frameworks of binary opposition may not be that surprising given the way in which globalization is often deployed simplistically as "'homogenization' versus 'heterogeneity,' 'uniformity' versus 'diversity,' 'cosmopolitanism' versus 'localism,' 'centralization' versus 'decentralization,' and so forth" (McCarthy et al., 2007, p. xix). Within this framing of globalization, the nation state is conceived as a fixed container of social relations that has clear boundaries dividing the inside from the outside. These frameworks also tend to rely on taken for granted assumptions about the nation state as a clearly defined and demarcated territory, in which the state has exclusive control over its people united by a common cultural set of traditions and history. Much of this work tends to overlook the tensions, contradictions and consistent negotiations involved in the overlap of political spaces and networks that reach across local, regional, national, supranational and global contexts in favor of simplistic binary opposition frameworks.

It is often the case that models used to assess issues of education policy shifts in governance have continued to hold up similar binary oppositions. These analyses generally followed a center-periphery or margin-center model, which propose as an underlying assumption that the central government acts as a central power force over the less powerful peripheries, maintained from a distance. In other work, I have traced the development of center-periphery or margin-center models, found in a diverse body of research, for example from Amin's (1980) work on the economic development of nation states to Brassloff's (1996) analysis on language and regional nationalism (Engel, 2008). In what is now considered widely as a contemporary era of globalization, these frameworks carry particular assumptions. For example, these frameworks often inappropriately assume that the periphery is at a distance from the power center, thus implying a level of passive disadvantage for the periphery.

Research on Spain has been not been immune to these frameworks. Rather, the center-periphery model has remained pervasive in studies of Spanish governance, politics, linguistic and education policy, and particularly in studies of educational decentralization (Brassloff, 1996; Hanson, 1998). According to these models, the Spanish central state becomes the assumed power center over the less powerful and historically marginalized regions. Governments (national and regional) are considered to be the sole actors in education policy formation processes. Educational decentralization, as a result, is assumed to be produced and enacted by the center.

In the literature focused on political and educational decentralization, Spain emerges as a central case of study. Spain has long been considered a miracle model, not only for its transition to democracy, but also for the massive restructuring of education governance within the national context (Brassloff, 1996; Corner, 1988; Hanson, 1998; Moreno, 2002). However, the frameworks that have been used to frame the Spanish case of decentralization, democratization and Europeanization appear to be wholly outdated. In the study of education governance, I found that the traditional ways in which education decentralization were being studied, in particular in a nation state context such as Spain, showed education policy being produced in a self-contained, hermitically sealed space, absent of the broader dynamics and complexities involved. In essentializing education policy formation into a linear, top-down model, it largely overlooks the tensions, contradictions, and consistent negotiations involved in the overlap of political spaces, out of which social and education policy is produced.

Scale

At the center of many of these shifts are concepts of scale and rescaling. Scale and processes of rescaling have now "attracted unprecedented methodological and empirical attention in the context of contemporary debates about globalization, shifting global-local relations, the reterritorialization of labor regulation, the apparent crisis of the Keynesian welfare national state, and urban-regional restructuring" (Brenner, 2001, p. 591). The term scale is purposefully used in this book to signify the dynamic, embryonic, and highly debated changes occurring in the reconfiguration of and relations across global, supranational, national, regional, and local spaces. This conception follows the work of Brenner (2001) who sought to "investigate the contested, and continually evolving, role of scale as a container, arena, scaffolding and hierarchy of sociospatial practices within contemporary capitalism" (p. 592). As scale is socially and politically constructed, processes of rescaling refer to the ways in which political, territorial, and economic configurations are broken down and remade.

The concept of rescaling is used to encompass trends that involve the layering of governance across various political spaces that are not automatically situated within state functions. This has important methodological implications as the focus of conceptualization is on the process of spatial reconfiguration, such as in the case of globalization and regionalization, rather than treating these developments as end products or outcomes (Brenner, 2004). Notions of scale and rescaling are useful for an examination of new modes of governance produced in education. As Robertson, Bonal, and Dale (2002) argued, "shifts in scale and processes of reterritorialization... are recognizable at the current time as strategies such as devolution, centralization, regionalization, decentralization, internationalization, and so on" (p. 476). These new shifts of governance appear to be the state's strategic responses to its consistent negotiation and intersection of numerous pressures from above and internal pressures from below.

As a result, processes of education policy production are becoming increasingly complex, layered, and hybridized, given the myriad of pressures emanating from global, supranational, national, regional, and local scales. This raises critical questions about the nature of education policy production, not only in light of an understanding of the state's role in developing policy, but also of policy production from within the overlap of political scales. In this line of inquiry, notions of scale and processes of rescaling appear particularly constructive as they initiate a disruption of the binary oppositions that often have been used to capture the multidimensional processes underlying shifts in decentralization. Processes of rescaling are illuminated in examples of recent education policy developments in Spain.

SPAIN AND CATALONIA

The book draws on a case of modern 20th and 21st century Spain. Spain is a unique case, as it has long been considered a successful "miracle" model for its rapid and relatively peaceful transition to democratization, decentralization and for its transition into one of the EU's core democracies. On issues of governance, Spain is one of the most politically, administratively and educationally decentralized states in Europe. The drastic process of unrolling the highly centralized, authoritarian state of the Francoist era (1939-1975) to the current democratic State of Autonomies is a significant case of education policy formation. Of particular importance is that educational governance in Spain, particularly decentralization, has been part of larger processes of nation-state reformation and the rebirth of the Spanish state. Against theories of globalization and the nation state, the case of Spain is a unique example of changes happening in the rest of Europe, and offers an interesting lens into larger issues of globalization, nation state restructuring and education policy formation.

In order to look more closely at devolution and regionalization in Europe, and to examine issues of globalization and Europeanization from outside a nation state perspective, the region of Catalonia, is highlighted as a way of grounding analysis. Catalonia possesses a long history of political alignment and struggle with powerful states of Western Europe, namely Spain and France. In its loss of independence to Spain in the 18th century, Catalonia has continued its quest for greater self-government and recognition of its national identity, separate from that of the Spanish state. Established in 1978 as one of the historical nations in the new, democratic and decentralized Spanish State of Autonomies, Catalonia has traditionally played a strong role in the central state realm. In the continued democratization and decentralization process of the past three decades, Catalonia has persistently pressed for the political recognition of a Catalan nation and a plurinational Spanish state.

Guibernau (1999) referred to Catalonia as a nation without a state. This signifies a "cultural communit[y] sharing a common past, attached to a clearly demarcated territory," but aims to "decide upon [its] political future which lack a state of [its] own" (p. 1). According to this perspective, Catalonia represents a collective political actor that retains a cultural and historical basis for its quest for greater autonomy and in some cases, independence. For Guibernau (1999), nations without states "are included within one or more states which they tend to regard as alien, and assert the right to self-determination, sometimes understood as further autonomy within the state, though, in other cases it involves the right to secession" (p. 2). In the context of the EU and EU Studies literature, Catalonia often has been referred to as a region. The EU's and EU Studies' use of the term region includes

> any piece of continuous territory, bigger than a mere locality or neighbourhood, which is part of the territory of a larger state (or states), and whose political authority or government…is subordinate to that of the state(s)….most such 'sub-state' regions, and particularly most regions defined in terms of political authority, have fallen wholly within the borders of a single state. (Anderson, 2001, p. 38)

It is significant to explore how concepts of nation, state and region are deployed and constructed differently in different spatial arenas. For example, there is mounting evidence that nations without states are becoming increasingly significant in EU politics, as they look to the EU as a viable means of gaining political recognition and act as key players in the project of European integration (Applegate, 1999; Giordano & Roller, 2002; Roller, 2004).

Catalonia is one key example. In the larger context of Europe, Catalonia is one of the most economically, politically and culturally powerful regions. Catalonia has been very much in favor of the EU promotion of regional strength. In 1986, when Spain joined the EU, Catalonia was a driving force in bringing attention to the political and economic importance of regions in the EU, as a way forward for economic development, social welfare and social inclusion. Catalonia remains a presence in Brussels in present day, as it was among the first of the Autonomous Communities of Spain to establish a regional office in Brussels independent of the Spanish state (Engel & Ortloff, 2009).

Just as Catalonia endorses the EU as a means for greater autonomy and recognition outside the Spanish state, the EU in turn has emphasized decentralization and the utilization of its local levels, cities, and regions for greater European integration and pursuit of greater economic growth. Some scholars have argued that the EU's emphasis on decentralization and regional governance demonstrates a political and ideological shift towards a "Europe of the Regions," in which regions acquire "greater protagonism in the political, economic, social and cultural arenas," ultimately disrupting the power of the nation state within the EU (Borrás-Alomar, Christiansen, & Rodríguez-Pose, 1994, p. 28). MacLeod (1999) has referred to the increased authorities of regions within the EU as Euro-regionalism.

NEW STATE FORMATIONS AND EDUCATION POLICY

From these shifts, it appears that in the rescaling of the state, traditional governance relations between regions, nation states, and supranational entities are being reconstituted. Consequently, the production of education policy is occurring within "a form of 'territorial complexity' defined by the interaction of four levels of government (EU, national, regional or local)" (Closa & Heywood, 2004, p. 86). Even with this recognition, much of the work retains dominant tendencies of deploying globalization and framing the configuration of the nation state in education. Saskia Sassen (2006) has noted that to study globalization and its implications, we have to "engage the most complex institutional architecture we have ever produced: the national state" (p. 1). However, Sassen (2006) went on to argue that much of the literature on globalization "leads to comparisons of the national and the global and easily falls into the trap of assuming that if the global exists it is in spite of the national" again relying on binary opposition frameworks (p. 9). By bringing Catalonia into the analysis of Spanish education policy, this book focuses on the nature of global transformations in educational governance by "moving inside the national state apparatus as it becomes the site of its own partial disassembling" (Sassen, 2006, p. 10). Ultimately, Catalonia provides an in-depth and rich perspective into the current status of the nation state transformations from below, and still maintains a focus on the nature of EU and global policy influences from above. This has led to an intersection, and perhaps clash, of regional, nation state, supranational and global education priorities.

The book's central argument is that education policy formation of governance, and specifically decentralization, needs to be conceptualized in such a way that highlights the various policy pressures and conflicting aims that emanate from multilevel contexts and diverse system actors. The tensions inherent in education policy production in Spain highlight the larger policy processes at play, which include various system actors, conflicting tensions, and contextual factors. While concepts such as nationalism, the nation state, and regional nationalism have been discussed in the literature on education governance and education policy studies, there is little theorization about the overlap of local, regional, national, supranational, and global scales in relation to the production of policy. Therefore, there is a need to address contemporary education policy production in light of the overlap of political scales.

In the post-Franco era of democratization, with pressures from Catalan actors and new policy spaces being opened up from below and the integration of Spain in the EU and processes of globalization from above, Spanish education policy are being produced within a cross-section of multiscalar policy pressures. To illustrate some of these shifts in education policy formation, this book draws on research conducted in 2003-2007, which included fieldwork research in three settings: Barcelona, Madrid, and Brussels (Engel, 2007a). This study is situated in the front-end stages of education policy, in which the agencies and multiple perspectives of policy actors are significant.

This study included data from over 40 semi-structured interviews with policy-makers, government officials, representatives of education agencies, key education experts, Ministers of Education, and Department of Education officials in Barcelona and Madrid, as well as key policy analysts and representatives of the OECD and the European Commission. Interviews centered on individual system agents' perceptions and experiences with contemporary education policy production, their views towards recent shifts in the production of education policy, and attitudes towards the development of local, regional, national, EU, and global processes in education. In this book, all direct quotes from participants are referred to as personal communications. I have refrained from including a date to ensure anonymity and confidentiality. Key policy documents were also collected and analyzed from each research site as key sources of information on the production of education policy and education policy debates. These documents included official, public documents generated by EU institutions, what was known in this period as the central Ministry of Education and Science (MEC) in Spain, and the Department of Education in Catalonia.

In addition to the uniqueness and complexity of the shifting policies of decentralization, what has drawn me to this particular case of study is that it is situated within a long and historical process of dramatic change: in Catalonia, the Spanish state, and the current EU project. The period of conducting fieldwork research was no exception to this dynamism. The fieldwork research began just a short time after the bombing in Madrid, which was followed by extensive political mobilization of Spanish citizens. During the summer of 2006, the Catalan government underwent a major change, with the ERC (Republican Left of Catalonia) party leaving the Tripartit, a three party left-wing political coalition consisting of the PSC (Socialist Party of Catalonia-Spanish Socialist Workers' Party), ERC, and ICV-EUiA (Green Initiative for Catalonia-United and Alternative Left). This political shift replaced some of the policy-makers, officials, and education authorities in the Department of Education in Catalonia. Also in 2006 was the process of revision of Catalonia's Statute of Autonomy, marking an increase in Catalan autonomy over decision-making and tense debate about language rights and rights of self-government. The revised Statute was approved by popular vote in June of 2006.

Education, during the period of fieldwork research, was also rife with political shifts and policy changes. The National Pact of Education of Catalonia was signed in 2006, laying the groundwork for what may be Catalonia's first education law. The newest stage in the trail of central state education legislation (the Organic Law of Education, also known as the LOE) was also approved and brought into force under the Socialist Party in May of 2006. These major political shifts and changes made it a significant time to conduct research on education policy formation, as each of these political efforts indicated and possessed a range of social, cultural, economic, and education implications. As Ronald Fraser (1994) expressed, "it was a privileged moment" to capture the perspectives, viewpoints, and experiences of individuals living, engaging, articulating, and creating these processes. This book then is to a certain extent looking back to the changes that have occurred since the transition to democracy and their implications for educational governance, for education policy production and for the future of education in Catalonia, Spain and the new Europe. In this way, this book offers as a glimpse into these sometimes drastic and considerably complex changes that underlie education policy production in the 21st century, globalized world.

THE CHAPTERS

New State Formations consists of six chapters, reflecting an interdisciplinary perspective on education reform, education policy, educational governance, global studies and education, and EU studies. Chapter 2, *Globalization and State Formations* introduces and lays out the major threads of the arguments, introducing a number of key concepts, including globalization, nation state, and governance, drawn from interdisciplinary scholarship in international and comparative education, critical geography, cultural studies and sociology. In particular, this chapter situates education and education policy within a broader framework of globalization and state transformation. That is, as global processes intensify, the state is being reshaped by pressures of convergence and divergence, resulting in the reconfiguration of education policy, especially related to education governance.

Chapter 3, *Constructing the New Spanish State* provides an overview of the historical and contemporary political shifts in Spain leading to the current democratized State of Autonomies. I foreground an analysis of education in the Francoist state (1939-1975), and the development of Spain's first modern mass education system in the post-Franco era. The latter half of the chapter explores the political, linguistic, and cultural claims of autonomy in Catalonia and the role of Catalonia in the democratization and decentralization of the new Spanish State.

The remaining chapters are conceptually organized to move from micro to macro views. Chapter 4, *Decentralization in the Post-Franco Era*, focuses on the changing territorial shape and political organization of the Spanish state, and its impact on education reform and policy in the autonomous community of Catalonia.

In this chapter, I highlight the struggles for education autonomy through complex intersections of language and culture extending across national and regional scales. In Chapter 5, *Global Pressures and EU Education Priorities*, I examine the EU as a significant education actor, largely the result of the development of new supranational policy instruments, and the relationship between education and the EU's continuous construction of a system "united in diversity" (Morely & Robins, 1995). The primary focus of this chapter is the continued development of a European education policy space, which in combination with new regionalisms has left public systems of education situated within a multilateral crossfire of diverse and often contrasting aims of education. As a result, education policies are being produced within a complex intersection of multiscalar policy pressures and challenging the dominant frameworks and concepts often deployed in comparative and international education.

The final chapter, Chapter 6, *Rescaling and the Politics of Decentralization* aims to tie in Chapters Four and Five, in order to provide a perspective into the interaction of pressures of global integration and regional nationalism as a form of state fragmentation. In this chapter, I highlight the emergence of a multiscalar political order that is shaping how policies of education decentralization are produced and how education systems are organized. This presses for new ways of framing education governance structures, given the disruption of the very language of decentralization and centralization. This chapter aims to press forward with a multiscalar understanding of educational governance in order to better understand the complexities involved in policy-making processes. As the states and regions of Europe continue to shift and reconfigure in the contemporary global era, the implications of these shifts for Europe and how we come to understand education governance become especially significant.

There still remains much more to the story of Catalonia, Spain and the new Europe than is possible to be covered in one book. Yet, in a context of substantial expansion of literature on globalization, the primary aim of the book is to show that no longer can policy be framed as a depoliticized output of a static and fixed state. While many scholars remain focused on the impact of globalization on the nation state, this book reaches beyond the state-centrism to examine the overlap of regional, national, EU, and global scales as they intersect in education policy production. In constructing a book around such a case study, the reality is that it can only ever capture just one snapshot of what is a long, dynamic history of Catalonia, Spain and the new Europe.

However, it is within the fragments and cracks that open up as a result of these changes and shifts that allow for a better understanding of the broader social and education transformations that occur as a result of global processes. Ultimately, while the dynamic changes occurring in Catalonia, Spain and Europe have shaped the experience and final construction of the book, it is important not to view this case as separate from the ebbs and flows of a long-standing history of dramatic historical, political, economic, cultural and education change. Rather, what is presented is a snapshot of one spatial and temporal point in time, providing insight into perhaps the futures of education policy formation in the 21st century.

GLOBALIZATION AND STATE FORMATIONS

We are living through epochal transformation, one as yet young but already showing its muscle.
(Sassen, 2006, p. 1)

Undeniably, globalization has become what Nòvoa (2002) has called "planet speak." While debates about globalization have not led to a single, universally accepted definition, there have been major strides in the social sciences to develop an understanding of the nature and scope of global forces. For some theorists, globalization is not simply ideological, nor a replacement term for Western imperialism or Americanization. Instead, globalization "reflects real structural changes in the scale of modern social organization" (Held & McGrew, 2003, p. 6). As evidenced by the vast literature and popular discourse, globalization has been used to capture many of the profound economic, political, social, cultural, technological, and educational changes in society.

Given the extensive body of literature, globalization, much like other conceptual terrains, has been subject to the development of neat divisions and binaries (Burawoy et al., 2000). Popular labels, such as skeptics, radicals, enthusiasts, hyper-globalists, and transformationalists have been used to give order and neatly carve out camp divisions in the debate surrounding globalization (Held & McGrew, 2003). While systematically outlining several perspectives out of the extensive cache of positions on globalization, these labels are neither adequate nor universally accepted. In Burawoy et al.'s (2000) argument for a more "grounded globalization," the authors dismissed these categorized camps as oversimplified and reductionist, as the "division into skeptics and radicals deftly forecloses other options" (p. 33). Furthermore, as Held and McGrew (2003) have addressed in their work, the divisions do not allow for an adequate perspective on the overlap across these positions. In other words, not all perspectives on globalization can be parceled out to one of these approaches.

This chapter approaches the discussion of globalization, and its impact on the nation state, educational governance, and introduces a discussion of decentralization. Rather than utilize pre-existing frameworks and camp divisions, such as those outlined above, this chapter first provides a brief overview of the literature on contemporary global processes. It then turns to a conceptual framework for understanding the modern nation state within the current round of globalization, followed by a section on the role of education in nation state building. In the last section, I explore the impact of global pressures on education, and some of the implications for educational governance. I argue that educational governance has become situated at the forefront of a wave of public sector reform that has been transformed under the rubric of New Public Management (NPM). This includes rhetoric of good governance, which is reshaping current policies of decentralization. The final section explores these reforms, establishing a framework of three forms of decentralization: political, administrative, and fiscal.

GLOBALIZATION: DEBATES AND INTERPRETATIONS

Held and McGrew's (2003) comprehensive approach to globalization has focused on its multiple dimension, which are economic, political, and cultural in nature. The authors argued that new modes of production in the economic realm, new developments of governance and a changing role of the state, as well as new configurations of cultural interrelationships characterize the present round of globalization. These divisions are not to be considered as strictly independent categories, as globalization is understood as "a set of mutually reinforcing transformations that are occurring more or less simultaneously" (Cohen & Kennedy, 2000, p. 24). Across these directives, global transformations are thought to be steered by technological advancements, the development of a single global economy, changing modes of production and nature of work, and fast capitalism. The argument follows that the development of a global economy has altered flows of capital, the development of transnational players in the global market place, and the different demands for a flexible, easily adaptable, multi-skilled workforce.

Through a historical lens, scholars see the contemporary round of globalization as much different from past economic developments, particularly as a consequence of the integration of the world's triad of regional economic powers into a single global economy (Dicken, 2003). The new global economy has pronounced flexibility and fluidity, "with multiple lines of power and decision-making mechanisms, analogous to a spider's web, as opposed to the static pyramidal organization of power that characterized the traditional capitalist system" (Morrow & Torres, 2000, p. 30). Rapid developments of a transnational economy, as the new global economy consists of networks of "informationalism" forged worldwide (Castells, 1996).

In the development of a single global economy, the core players have moved into a different organization, shifts in production, and underlying focus of work (Harvey, 1989). The Fordist era of mass industrialization, manufacturing, and Frederick Taylor's scientific management (Taylorization) progressively developed from the turn of the 20th century to the early 1970s. The new post-Fordist era of flexible, multi-skilled labor values flexibility, instantaneity, and rapidity, which have replaced the rigid structure and organization of the Fordist economy (Harvey, 1989). Aside from the increase of service and white-collar sectors, the post-Fordist economy has increased the feminization of specific work forces, in which employers seeking to cheapen their costs of labor look towards the hiring of women (Blackmore, 2000). These economic manifestations of globalization are interrelated and deeply linked with political dimensions of globalization.

These global economic transformations have spurred new conceptions of governance and disrupted the territorial, political, and economic stronghold of the state in political and policy-making processes. This is related to an increasingly crowded policy stage, given the recent "multiplication of all kinds of governance" (Rosenau, 2003, p. 230). This includes various institutions of the state apparatus, international organizations (IOs), such as the Organization for Economic Co-operation and Development (OECD), the United Nations Educational, Scientific and Cultural Organization (UNESCO), the International Monetary Fund (IMF), and the World Bank, as well as supranational entities, such as the EU.

Ranging from major donors, such as the World Bank, and the IMF's new role in the more recent (2009) G20 global stimulus plan, to the development of global (performance) indicators and benchmarks, such as the work of the OECD, each of these organizations are important to understanding political globalization and the numerous pressures facing nation state systems. As Iriye (2004) argued, with such a rise in power of IOs, "the contemporary world would be incomprehensible without taking them into consideration" (p. 1). Indeed, researchers in the social sciences continue to explore the nature and the role, as well as the impact of IOs in both policy development and implementation.

For example, Dale and Robertson (2002) compared the EU, Asia-Pacific Economic Cooperation (APEC) and North Atlantic Free Trade Agreement (NAFTA). Henry et al. (2001) critically examined the OECD, while Jones (1998) discussed the World Bank in contrast with United Nations Children's Fund (UNICEF) and UNESCO. Rutkowski (2007) examined the growth, completion and implications of the World Educational Indicators (WEI) project, undertaken by several IOs. In his work, Rutkowski (2007) explored the ways in which indicators were developed and used by IOs, as well as their implications for globalization and policy steering in nation state social and economic development and national educational systems.

Through these and other examples, it becomes apparent that IOs have aided the development of powerful global networks that circulate particular ideas and ideologies around the world. Influential organizations like the World Bank and OECD widely purport ideas and ideologies linked with neoliberal economic globalization, such as for example the Washington Consensus. The term Washington Consensus has often been used to represent neoliberal globalization and neoliberal policy. It originally was developed by John Williamson (1990) in the promotion of a series of ten reforms, which were discussed in the World Bank Annual World Poverty Report (2000). Central to the Washington Consensus is the attention given to the efficiency of public services and resources, with adequate systems of accountability, which the IMF has in the past referred to in terms of transparency of financial markets and the World Bank has described as good governance, in its concern with enhancing accountability within economies. This has particular implications for driving a particular market-driven approach to governance.

Theories of globalization have also explored the impact of the rapid movement of people, ideas, and cultural communication worldwide, disrupting assumptions about the tight relationship between the nation state, and culture and identity. The literature on cultural globalization includes arguments ranging from increased global interconnectedness, cosmopolitanism, and homogeneity to new forms of cultural imperialism, cultural difference, and hybridization (Appadurai, 1996; Burawoy et al., 2000; Nederveen Pieterse, 2004a). From Samuel Huntington's (1996) *Clash of civilizations* to Benjamin Barber's (1996) *Jihad vs. McWorld*, cultural difference has been as much a part of the globalization debates as analyses of world interconnectedness and cosmopolitanism (Nederveen Pieterse, 2004a; Nussbaum, 1996). Notwithstanding the interconnectedness and interdependency of the 21st century, globalized world, global mobility and access are certainly by no means equal or equitable, as shown in Bauman's (1998) analysis of travelers and vagabonds.

The ways in which globalization affects nation states with respect to processes of both integration and fragmentation is not uniform across countries. Rather these processes operate in a highly complex fashion, as they "operate in a contradictory or oppositional fashion" (Giddens, 1999, http://news.bbc.co.uk/hi/english/static/events/reith_99/week1/week1.htm, para. 18). For example, the new challenges and needs of the global economy often demand the reinforcement of new actors and governance structures, which will be discussed further below. What is significant is that often these new demands are linked with new cultural identity formations through the revival of local and regional cultural identities and sensibilities. Moreover, as will be highlighted in the case of Catalonia and Spain, the increase in global mobility and the resulting enhancement of cultural diversity within societies poses significant challenges for nation state governance structures and democratic state arrangements.

WEAK-STATE VS. STRONG-STATE

Implicit in most debates and interpretations of globalization is the nation state. Here, it is helpful to outline some basic definitions of nation, state, and the nation state. In an examination of these three complex concepts, the nation state appears to exist as an imposed set of boundaries, in which cultural and political divisions often do not neatly align (Kellas, 2004). In this area of interest, scholars have worked towards an understanding of both nation and state. This literature is too robust to do justice to all of the varying perspectives and developments. However, to draw from one example, Benyon and Dunkerly (2000) distinguished the nation from the state:

> Nations are composed of groups whose common identity is based on generally shared belief in a core notion of nationhood; and these constructions of nationhood appear to be steadily increasing and are regularly crossing state boundaries. In the 'new global order', nations and states are often in conflict in that more and more 'nations' appear to be threatened with disintegration. (p. 5)

Examples of the mass nationalism movement to build "imagined communities" (Anderson, 1983) within states, as well as complications of nations without states, (Guibernau, 1999) include the Catalan and Basque of Spain, the Quebecois of Canada, East Timoreans, Palestinians, Kurds, and indigenous people in Chiapas, among others (Dicken, 2003). These movements have to be seen in light of the complex process of constructing the nation state.

Complicating the literature on the nation state, nation, and state even more is the use of concepts, such as regions, regional nations, sub-nations and sub-states. Kellas (2004) argued "apart from states there are substate regional political units within federal and devolved states," going on to write, "many [substate regions] are national in character and...owe their political status to nationalism" (p. 5). Yet, it is often the considered that "states are legitimate only to the extent that they are 'nation-states'" (Kellas, 2004, p. 6). This idea of nation state legitimacy is based on the development of the modern state, which consisted of a sovereign political unit built around a common cultural identity. It is over centuries that states have constructed nationhood.

The modern state, initiated with the 1648 Treaty of Westphalia, and massively developed in the 19th century, refers to the realization of sovereignty over particular state territory, the building of state institutions and infrastructure, and the binding of citizens under a constructed common national identity (Green, 1997). In this sense, it signifies one national community governed by a single state apparatus. The concept, nation state, is assumed to imply "citizen population[s] plus political state" apparatus (Green, 1997, p. 31). It needs to be recognized however, that both the nation and the state are socially and politically constructed and that the development of both the nation and the state include a history of are intense conflicts and tensions.

Most central to many of the globalization debates and interpretations emerging in the 1990s is the apparent disruption globalization has caused in the traditional ways in which the nation state has been conceived of and framed. This ultimately led to a questioning of a number of long-held assumptions of the state and its role in policy formation. As opposed to internationalization, in which the state is a primary unit of analysis in bilateral and multilateral exchanges, globalization assumes a significantly different conception of the state (Taylor et al., 1997). Globalization extends beyond international relations and suggests not only cross-border, but trans-border flows, supraterritoriality, supranational entities, deterritorialization, where for example "'place' is not territorially fixed, territorial distance is covered in effectively no time, and territorial boundaries present no particular impediment" (Scholte, 2000, p. 48). This theoretical account pinpoints transnational and supranational organizations as economic players.

Furthermore, it holds that an extension of economic structures and interactions goes well beyond the nation state, disrupting the assumed substance, power, and territorial strong-hold of the state. According to this view, governance is no longer directly fixed to the state "as a static block, platform, or container" (Brenner, 2004, p. 29). Rather, as states face the demands of the new global economy, the exclusive connection between territory and political power appears to have been broken. This is suggested by the "retreat and erosion" (Strange, 1996), "the hollowing out" (Jessop, 1999), the "changing architecture" (Cerny, 1990) of the state. These debates and interpretations are central, as while there have been other perspectives, especially ones emerging more recently, the debates about the global and the nation state that emerged in the 1990s are still central in framing concepts and issues within the study of globalization and education.

The general argument of what can be referred to as weak-state theories proposed that the erosion of the state and its borders are a consequence of multi-lateral policy production, as well as the global economy, the rise in region states (Payne, 2003), supranational economies (Ohmae, 1995), the pooling of sovereignty (Robertson, 1992), and internal fragmentation (Benyon & Dunkerly, 2000; Nederveen Pieterse, 2004a). This perspective of the state and global processes includes the argument that "national boundaries no longer act as 'watertight' containers of the production process" (Dicken, 2003, p. 9). For example, in Appaduari's (1996) concept of scapes and flows, he argued that modernity has lost its grip on the nation state by way of transnational mobility, global informationalism, and the media. Similarly, Burawoy et al. (2000) reasoned that

> as civil society loses its influence over the state, it turns outward, developing what we have called *transnational* connections—flows of people, information, and ideas, and the stretching of organizations, identities, and families. The dense ties that once connected civil society to the state are being detached and redirected across national boundaries to form a thickening global public sphere. (p. 34)

According to these weak-state views emerging in the 1990s, the nation state's territorial, economic, and political stronghold had become dismantled.

Within these weak-state arguments, global processes are seen to have eased and opened up spaces for developing and asserting nationalist claims. For example, Giddens (1999) argued that global processes have led not only to the breakdown of nation states by pressures of integration, but also of fragmentation. As particular entities, regions now actively seek to recapture autonomy over areas of governance on the basis of historically rooted nationalism, leading to debates over independence, separatism, federalism, autonomy, and decentralization within the nation state system. Giddens (1999) has argued that in recent years, these movements are predominantly the result of "globalising tendencies, as the hold of older nation states weakens," pointing out that new transnational spaces have opened up, creating new cultural identities in their wake (http://news.bbc.co.uk/hi/english/static/events/reith_99/week1/week1.htm, para. 19).

While weak-state theories have pointed to the erosion of the state, other accounts, which I have referred to elsewhere as strong-state theories, have viewed the role of the state in a much different light. Strong-state theories have tended to explore some political, economic, and cultural transformations that have occurred with globalization. However, these views typically have assumed that these alterations do not suggest the kind of dramatic and radical changes to the state that the weak-state theorists have claimed. Rather, changes in the state, it has been believed, could be more readily attributed to internationalization. In a focus on internationalization, the state is the central point of governance and policy formation within cross-border exchanges. Within strong-state analyses, there also has been a retention and validation of territorially defined units of analysis. The strong-state position has examined cultural trends in a similar fashion, arguing that there has been a rejuvenation of nationalist sensibilities and patriotism, such as during the period immediately following September 11, 2001 in the US, rather than the development of a global popular culture or exceeding cultural fragmentation.

Some strong-state theorists have rejected the very discourse of globalization as a part and parcel of a larger ideological myth. Globalization, for Hirst and Thompson (1996), was nothing more than rhetorical "globaloney" and went on to problematize the ahistorical position offered by globalization theories. Strong-state theorists, such as Frank (1998) and Hirst and Thompson (1996) have cited historical quantitative data of the global movement of trade and people. Based on these data, authors argued that as early as the 19th century the world experienced increased mobility of people through massive migration patterns, as well as urbanization and the development of global city centers. Following this line, some scholars have argued that this historical period was more open in terms of international trade and mobility than the contemporary period.

In addition, strong-state theorists often have argued that what the hyper-globalists label as globalization is in fact not a recent phenomenon. Wallerstein (2000), in his development of world-systems theory, pointedly stated, "the processes that are usually meant when we speak of globalization are not in fact new at all. They have existed for some 500 years" (p. 250). He pointed out what he pinned as historical crises and moments of transformation. Other positions hold that Oriental globalization and imperialism theories need to be included as antecedents or predecessors of the contemporary round of globalization (Frank, 1998). When taking these arguments and debates into account, a view emerges that "globalization is a long-term historical process of growing worldwide interconnectedness" (Nederveen Pieterse, 1995, p. 45). What is significant here is that globalization can be understood as part of a contemporary round of intense changes, markedly different from earlier periods, but nonetheless possessing historical roots. While globalization debates about the impact and the fate of the nation state raged during the 1990s, strong-state and weak-state perspectives continue to be represented in present day. For example, the new global significance of the IMF, once thought to be declining in influence, may represent more of a weak-state perspective, while strong-state views are represented by recent developments in certain countries to nationalize banks and develop individual national stimulus plans.

In the context of globalization theories, as exemplified by strong-state and weak-state theories, the nation state is showcased as the central agent or unit of analysis. As a result, much of the globalization literature has revolved around the nation state. It is worth noting that in the conception of social science disciplines in the 19th century, the nation state was the assumed, natural reference point. Nation state systems, as bounded territorial units, historically provided the primary units of analysis. In many disciplines today, this remains the case, as "conventional ideas of research in the social sciences and humanities are often implicitly if sometimes subtly connected in some way or another to the nation state" (Kenway & Fahey, 2009, p. 14). This has often lent itself to rather state-centric assumptions.

Brenner (2004) has synthesized three assumptions of state-centrism in the social sciences: First, state-centrism assumes an ahistorical timelessness of social space, which he has referred to as "spatial fetishism." Second, state-centrism assumes the state to be a tightly bounded and organized territorial container, also referred to as "methodological territorialism" (Dale, 2005; Scholte, 2000), which places territoriality as a center determinant of social relations. Third, state-centrism assumes "methodological nationalism," in which the national scale is the primary agent of the social. Brenner (2004) argued that the three assumptions about the state together "generate an internalist model of societal development in which national territoriality is presumed to operate as a static, fixed, and timeless container of historicity" (p. 38). As I argue in this book, education is no exception to the pervasive state-centrism of the social sciences, which may not be surprising given education's historical role in the building of the modern nation state system.

CONSTRUCTING THE NATION STATE

Globalization is altering national systems of education in such a way that education is undergoing a fundamental reformation to meet the needs of the global economy (Burbules & Torres, 2000). Taylor et al. (1997) suggested that the state is central to an understanding of multiple policy processes and the complex power relationships at play. However, the authors argued

> the state is not a not a unitary entity to which can be ascribed purposeful action, nor is it a straightforward instrument of powerful groups external to it such as transnational corporations. Rather, the state can be conceptualized as a set of processes which collectively have particular outcomes. Furthermore, the state consists of a large number of entities...which often have conflicting interests. (p. 29)

In the construction of the modern nation state system, education was utilized as a key mechanism. Breaking from family, church, and apprentice style education programs, new state public school systems were built as early as the 19th century to support the development of the modern nation state system. Horace Mann's Common School Movement in the US, as a new tax-supported form of education with centralized teacher-training programs and curriculum is one example of the 19th century development of a national public education system (Urban & Wagoner, 2003). National public systems of education were also taking place across modern European states and Japan (Green, 1997). Education for the general purpose of self-cultivation (education to enhance knowledge for knowledge's sake) was not a primary objective. Rather, education as an institution developed as an important agent for the purpose of nation state building with two distinct, yet ultimately intertwined motives: economic development and social cohesion. These dual purposes underline core state intervention and responsibility in education.

It is believed that these purposes are the two primary concerns of state function (accumulation and legitimation), outlined by the fundamental work of Claus Offe (1984). Through Offe's work, the state is seen as essentially charged with managing its economic infrastructure and citizens to avoid economic crisis through legitimating itself by means of gaining and maintaining mass loyalty. In this perspective, the state has regulated and intervened in its national education system according to traditional conceptions of the economic value of schooling and the creation of a competitive labor force. On the one hand then, education has served to create a core-trained workforce to sustain the building of an economic infrastructure. In addition, historically in nation states, education was often used as a tool to manage massive societal changes occurring, for example, urbanization, industrialization, or immigration. In reaction to societal changes such as these, public education systems became institutions to develop a skilled workforce to meet the demands of capital accumulation and to organize societies around particular national ideas, in attempts to legitimize the nation state.

In the development of the modern nation state system, education in the public sector was looked at as the "major instrument in the forging of national identity" (Green, 1997, p. 94). Education thus serves to build social cohesion, develop national coherence, and legitimate a sense of national identity among citizens and diverse communities. Modern nation state construction strategically has used public education in the building, sustaining, and "shap[ing itself] into an 'imagined community' of coherent modern identity through warfare, religion, blood, patriotic symbology, and language" (Wilson & Dissanayake, 1996, p. 3). In relation to the development of a state apparatus, as well as issues of identity and nationhood, education has played a role in the intertwined goals of the nation state: economic development and citizenry creation. However, these processes often have been filled with tension and at times, conflict.

Within the role of education in the construction of the nation state, there are a number of conflicting pressures that have informed a number of debates over policy content. Returning to Offe's (1984) theory of the dual state functions of capital accumulation and legitimation, Bonal (2003) discussed an endemic tension, writing that "some of the attempts to meet the accumulation goal would usually be accompanied by an effect of undermining the state's legitimation capacity" (p. 161). Bonal (2003) wrote that the state was charged with creating and maintaining social cohesion, in particular to legitimate itself and sustain capital accumulation. In terms of social cohesion, the state carried responsibility for providing equal and equitable grounds for educational opportunity among diverse students and "effects of class, gender, and ethnic differences on educational performance" (Bonal, 2003, p. 162). The endemic tension then is that both the former and latter tasks have the potential to undermine the other.

In education, the former task of capital accumulation, in which one policy may be the selection and promotion of particular students for advanced levels of education and the overarching aim for excellence in schools has the possibility of undermining the latter task by "creating resistance and contestation from those excluded by the system" (Bonal, 2003, p. 161). Increasingly, policy agendas around the world have pressed for excellence and efficiency in education, as well as enhancing equality and social inclusion. Much has been written about the prioritizing of excellence, leading to exclusionary practices and social unrest rather than enhance goals of social cohesion. This contrast between excellence or efficiency and social inclusion and equality has continued in the contemporary post-Fordist globalization era. These varying aims of education are linked to the introduction of new educational players, namely IOs, which are developing and legitimating certain educational reforms, as well as forming new international measures of educational achievement, leading both to international benchmarking practices and ranking systems.

Linked to the discussion above, IOs, like the OECD, World Bank and the EU, now play a more significant part in education policy production, implementation and evaluation processes than ever before. For example, the OECD's work has been influential in guiding the ways in which education policy is being thought about in national systems around the world. The OECD's policy recommendations purport a particular "neo-liberal instrumentalist conception of education, viewed as a major factor in contributing to human capital formation and economic growth" (Rizvi & Lingard, 2006, p. 249). As Rizvi and Lingard (2006) have argued, the OECD's "educational policy work is widely used by national governments to guide their reform agendas. Its statistical compilations provide a reference point for benchmarking and for promoting policy debates" (p. 248). By shaping policy debates in education through "consensus-building," the OECD is able to influence the educational agendas of national governments around the world (Rizvi & Lingard, p. 248).

Another example of how IOs engage in the negotiation of consensus and conventions can be shown through the Bologna Declaration, which was developed by the EU to ensure coordinated policy action across national systems of education. The Bologna Process, as it often is called, began in 1999 with 29 countries signing the Bologna Declaration as a pledge to create a European space for higher education by 2010. To date, 46 countries now participate in the Bologna Process. It involves a number of educational reforms in order to make individual country's higher education systems compatible with one another. These reforms include a common framework for degrees, compatible undergraduate and postgraduate studies, harmonious credit systems, a common framework for quality assurance, and the enhancement of free mobility of students and teachers. These reforms have "compelled national policymakers to restructure their systems of higher education to ensure a fairer and more efficient system of credit transfer, enabling students to become more mobile across national systems…which is considered highly desirable for the global economy" (Rizvi & Lingard, p. 247).

IOs actively encourage international cooperation in education through the development of global indicators of performance and quality assurance. Increasingly, national governments and policy-makers look to cross-national studies of student academic achievement. Starting in the 1950s, IOs, such as UNESCO and the OECD "intensified the exchange and accumulation of data relating to the different patterns of educational organization, curricula, and teaching methods. There was a growing awareness of the role that formal education played in promoting – or hindering – social and economic development" (Postlethwaite, 1999, p. 7). Since the 1990s, comparative educational assessments of educational achievement have been developed at a rapid rate.

For example, the Programme for International Student Assessment (PISA) was developed by the OECD in order to compare 15-year old students' scholastic performance across national education systems. Two other well-known international educational assessments include Trends in International Mathematics and Science Study (TIMSS) and Progress in International Reading Literacy Study (PIRLS), both developed by the International Association for the Evaluation of Educational Achievement (IEA), a non-governmental, non-profit organization. These assessments have had an increasing number of countries participate. For example, since 1995, TIMSS has had over 50 countries participating in each study, which assesses 4th and 8th grade students' mathematics and science achievement in order to compare across countries. These assessments have become increasingly significant in the development of global performance indicators and benchmarks and the spread of so-called best practices in education.

Through these developments, and the powerful policy networks constructed by IOs, education policies are being exchanged and borrowed between national systems at an increasingly rapid rate. In Phillips and Ochs' (2003) study of policy borrowing in education, they looked specifically at "outward gazing" as means of networking certain policies and practices. In other work, Samoff (2003) aptly outlined the nature of the movement and exchange of global trends in education policy reform. He addressed the history of the development of policy borrowing, shaping, and imposing in education and outlined the various policy players that construct these relationships. Although policy occurs within this framework of exchange, influence, and imposition, the ways in which policy is negotiated and implemented is contingent on locality and site-specific contexts.

As pointed out by Steiner-Khamsi (2004), copying is not necessarily equated with borrowing. Rather, practices and processes of educational borrowing and lending reveals "processes of local adaptation, modification, and resistance to global forces in education" (p. 5). Nonetheless, as Samoff (2003) argued, through policy exchange, there has been "the broad adoption of a common framework for describing, categorizing, analyzing, and assessing education," leaving nation states under increasing pressure and coercion to take new policy developments into account (p. 62). This is particularly the case as the development of goals, benchmarks, and standards reinforces notions of global competition, the process of educational borrowing and lending, and pressure on national education systems to converge on notions of best practice and performance guidelines.

Additionally, the establishment of these recent trends in educational reform reveals the importance of considering the various actors involved in the spread of global imperatives for education. IOs and supranational organizations, such as the EU, often argue that their involvement in education is limited to the creation of a space in which national ministries and policy-makers can exchange educational ideas and best practices. However, in recent years, these organizations have developed their own independent positions on education and entered into policy debates as important actors in their own right (Rizvi & Lingard, 2006). Their ideas and ideologies about education have become increasingly prominent in nation state education policy priorities, often overshadowing local educational imperatives. This has effectively dismantled the exclusive relationship between the modern nation state system and education policy formation.

RECONFIGURING EDUCATIONAL GOVERNANCE

Globalization has sparked new developments in education policy, the politics of education, and reconfigurations of governance (Marginson, 1999). Morrow and Torres (2000) argued that there are three implications of globalization on education: the relationship between the state and the global economy and the ways in which the state is moving away from a Keynesian model; educational restructuring and reform as a result of neoliberal pressures; and imperatives of the global economy, such as its requirements for a flexible, competent workforce. These implications raise important questions about state intervention in education policy production and educational governance.

The force of globalization and rise of a post-Fordist economic organization has brought about a new set of challenges for the state, resulting in new mechanisms of state intervention in education policy production and what has been looked at as a widespread crisis of educational efficiency and effectiveness (Bonal, 2003; Cerny, 1990). In an era of globalization, much of what is regarded as educational reform is based on the conviction that education, particularly public education, is too ineffective and inefficient to meet the demands of global competition. This has featured widely in discourses of key educational reports of both nation state and IOs.

For example, the OECD's (1996) influential report, *The Knowledge Based Economy* pressed the economic goals of education as key priorities, underpinning the dominant idea that education is the key instrument for economic success in a competitive global marketplace. Dale (2000) argued, "education has been seen as the key factor in honing states' competitive edge with respect to each other, since in the new global economy human resources are much less 'footloose' than other kinds of resources" (p. 10). To be able to compete globally with other knowledge-based economies, as well as maintain an innovative, flexible supply of perennial workers, education has been targeted to bolster and advance a labor force and "up skill" populations suitable for the demands of the global economy.

The role of education as an economic investment refers to human capital theory. This is seen as an increase in stock of human capital, which helps to advance potential economic developments and innovation (Becker, 1964). The OECD's (1998) report entitled, *Human Capital Investment: An International Comparison*, it has been argued that

> The level of skills, knowledge and competencies held at any one time by individuals can be taken to represent the 'stock' of human capital. The total stock within a country can influence its prosperity and international competitiveness. The distribution of knowledge and skills has an important bearing on social participation and access to employment and income. So, governments are interested in both the overall human capital stock and ways in which specific skills and competencies are distributed within the population. (p. 15)

Education therefore and its role in skill development has been a significant policy focus in education. Hartley (2003) defined the human capital focus specific to education "as an up-front investment which causes increasing rates of economic return to both the individual and society, the benefits to the latter being an aggregation of those to the former" (p. 444). In light of the reshaping of national education policy, the enhancement of human capital assists the state as a sound investment in capital accumulation.

As argued by Tickell and Peck (2003), neoliberalization and globalization have become entangled in one another. This has particularly been around the perspective that states have become enveloped in scaled-back, absentee forms. At its core, the theory of neoliberalism holds that heightened market relations and privatization stipulate a minimalist state aimed at advocating economic efficiency and productivity. Harvey (2005) has defined neoliberalism as:

> a theory of political economic practices that proposes that human well-being can best be advanced by liberating individual entrepreneurial freedoms and skills with an institutional framework characterized by strong private property rights, free markets, and free trade. The role of the state is to create and preserve an institutional framework appropriate to such practices....State interventions in markets (once created) must be kept to a bare minimum. (p. 2)

Theorists have often cited neoliberalism and neoliberal globalization as the underlying cause of the spread of the human capital rationale in education.

The 1980s rise of neoliberalism can be noted particularly in education in its application of structural adjustment program policies in New Zealand from 1984-1990 with the New Labor Government in power (Kelsey, 1995), the aggressive restructuring of public educational reform programs in Thatcher's England and in the first wave of Reagan deregulation in the 1980s (Nederveen Pieterse, 2004b, p. 11), as well as in Canada, Germany, the Netherlands, and France (Brenner & Theodore, 2002). The ideas underlying many of these reform movements represent a naturalization of market logics, new conceptions of governance based on a minimalist, deregulated state with a lean government, and the promotion of values, such as competition, economic efficiency, and choice. As Peck and Tickell (2002) have argued, neo-liberalism promotes and normalizes a "growth-first approach" to policy, making social welfare concerns secondary (p. 394). Influenced by these pressures, education and knowledge, which were traditionally thought of as highly national, are increasingly viewed as a sound investment to give states a global competitive edge.

Pressures of neoliberal globalization appear to be increasingly impacting the ways in which education policy is produced in relation to economic investment and efficiency. These pressures are represented in the various discourses and practices, most notably of IOs. Rutkowski (2007) argued "the relatively recent focus on human capital formation as an engine for economic growth within the global knowledge economy has put education squarely on the radar of international organizations" (p. 1-2). IOs, such as the OECD, have become active transporters of neoliberal agendas in education (Henry, Lingard, Rizvi & Taylor, 2001). As a result, discourses of accountability, standardization, transparency, outcomes-based assessments, and performance management in education are part and parcel to the global spread of the influential doctrine of New Public Management (NPM). NPM encompasses three main tenets: a reduction in public spending, in part through privatization and decentralization, stress on efficiency and output of public services, and construction of policy and implementation of public services geared much more towards global competition (Hood, 1991). An illustrative example is the OECD's (1995) influential report, *Governance in Transition: Public Management Reforms in OECD Countries*.

This report is perhaps one of the best examples of the NPM doctrine, outlined the shift in practices of effective management and governance, in which accountability, transparency, and decentralization, are argued to be central practices of what has been referred to as good governance. These trends represent what appears to be an overarching attempt to run the public sector, including education, more efficiently. This has sparked concern over the creation of the audit society, as embodying the convergence of accountability and outcomes-based measurement ideologies and practices of education (Power, 1997). In Kivinen and Nurmi's (2003) assessment of the promotion of marketization and performance-based policy trends, they argued that under the pressures of accountability, "the state is left with the double role of acting both as the sponsor and as the auditor who assesses output" (Kivinen & Nurmi, 2003, p. 84). Linked with the account-ability movement, decentralization has become a central governance strategy related to the deregulation of the state in the globalization era (Kamat, 2000; Karlsen, 2000).

Scholars have argued that in order to replace an all-authoritarian government, the central goal of states is the creation of "the self-regulating, choice-making, self-reliant individual" as a form of governance (Marginson, 1999, p. 25). Hay's (2003) work on neoliberalism, cultural technologies, and governing from a distance has been important as it critically intervenes in the work on neoliberalism, bringing in Foucault's conception of governmentality. Hay (2003) outlined his conception of the idea of governmentality, meaning how to govern over increasingly large populations and expanding territories, while satisfying the government's quest to "rely less upon political institutions of the state...and develop techniques for *governing at a distance*," which requires particular sets of rules for conduct (p. 165–166; author's italics). Hay (2003) wrote

> because a neoliberal form of governance assumes that social subjects are not and should not be subject to direct forms of state control, it relies upon mechanisms for governing 'through society,' through programs that shape, guide, channel—and upon *responsible*, self-disciplining social subjects. (p. 166; author's italics)

The mechanisms by which the state attempts to govern from a distance can be identified concretely by new modes of educational governance produced in the form of NPM, especially concerning decentralization. The following section explores this at greater length.

DECENTRALIZATION

New forms of governance have become a central topic in educational reform debates in systems around the world. The process of decentralization has been brought to the center of many debates and reform movements in education. Often, IOs have stressed the importance of decentralization as a central management technique. As one illustration, a World Bank (2005) report stated that

> the past decades have witnessed significant changes in the way legislation has been used to regulate education—changes in resource control and utilization, and movement toward the devolution and decentralization of school administration. New management practices at the central and local levels have been introduced to support the implementation of these changes. (p. 167–168)

Underlying reforms of educational governance are different, but fundamental aims of education, including the enhancement of social inclusion and equity. As an example, Mark Bray (1999) discussed issues surrounding educational governance as being about "matters of control, about the distribution of resources, and, in the education sector, about access to opportunities that can fundamentally influence the quality of life for both individual and social groups" (p. 227). One of the most promising and conflicting aspects of examining trends in educational decentralization involves its very usage and underlying meanings.

The most readily assumed view is that with decentralization, there is an increase in citizen participation, local control, a sense of bringing the government to the people, and an overall enhancement of democratic principles. However, neoliberal ideas and ideologies include an alternative definition of decentralization, which is underpinned by the essential belief that less central bureaucracy enhances system efficiency. Likewise, decentralization also may signify a strategy of fiscal management in order to ease the financial burden of the central state, generate greater public expenditure on education through the transfer of financial responsibilities to local and regional levels, and/or achieve greater efficiency in fiscal matters.

Whether about local voice, democracy or efficiency, these multiple meanings are often blurred into a single definition of decentralization as a transfer of educational responsibility and management from central to "subsidiary levels of government, such as states and municipalities" (Alexander, 2002, p. 27). Moreover, it is frequently the case that decentralization is used as "catch-all term for the granting of greater decision-making authority and autonomy" (OECD, 1995, p. 157). While there are a wide variety of uses of the term decentralization, the following three distinctions are helpful, as discussed in Rizvi et al. (2005):
- Political decentralization or devolution
- Administrative or functional decentralization
- Fiscal decentralization

The first definition, political decentralization or devolution, signifies that the central state transfers major decision-making power to regional and local or municipal levels.

In educational governance and management systems, when a form of political decentralization is advocated, it is often associated with efforts of democratization to maximize the participation of citizens (Hanson, 2000; Rizvi et al., 2005; Rondinelli, 1990). As such, political decentralization includes a promotion and reinforcement of democratic ideals, greater receptiveness to local needs, capabilities of addressing local problems, and empowerment at a community level (Astiz, Wiseman & Baker, 2002). The push towards political decentralization may also stem from pressures emanating from regional and local levels based on particular political histories and linguistic and cultural heritage. Examples of politically motivated decentralization include Papua New Guinea, the Philippines, Russia, and the Sudan (Bray & Mukundan, 2003).

With administrative or functional decentralization, there is a transfer of central agency responsibilities, managerial tasks, and funding allocations to local level government agencies (Hanson, 2000; Rizvi et al., 2005; Rondinelli, 1990). However, regional and local systems of educational governance are more likely to be steered from a distance, according to priorities of the central state and global pressures. One illustration, among others, is the New Labor era in England, in which education was decentralized; yet, important aspects, such as curriculum, standards, and evaluation policy decisions for example, have remained under the strict control of the central government (Biesta, 2004). Under this type of governance, local and regional educational systems are held to increased accountability standards by the central state.

Often efficiency in educational governance is the rationale for administrative decentralization. Fiske (1996) argued that the transfer of responsibilities to "regional or local levels will result in a more efficient system because it eliminates overlays of bureaucratic procedure and motivates education officials to be more productive" (p. 25). Advocated in the name of efficiency, administrative decentralization is often linked to technologies of accountability and transparency as a part of the broader notions of public management and/or good governance. Regional and local governments may experience an increase in their capabilities and competencies for governing and decision-making. However, these capabilities function within a particular context of unification, accountability, and work towards a set of standard benchmarks and goals dictated from a central administrative body. This is often linked to the changing needs of the central state, as well as its financial institutions.

In a post-Fordist economy in which employers seek to cheapen labor costs and governments are pressured to scale back on public service expenses, while looking to increase efficiency of these services, it is often the case that policy-makers advocate for new forms of governance. Kamat (2000) wrote

> decentralization portends a different configuration of state sociospatial organization to manage the precarious equilibrium of global capital trade, investment, and speculation. Such a configuration is one in which the state is at once decentered by opening the state to multiple other actors who must coordinate and conduct the everyday business of education and simultaneously, is strengthened by organizing the field of possibilities, and laying the boundaries for local policy. (p. 6–7)

The scaling-back of the state in the public sector has arguably had an impact on the decentralization of public education, often leaving fiscal and administrative responsibilities to regional, municipal, or local levels.

It is typically argued that in education policy reform efforts, administrative decentralization requires the application of a form of fiscal or financial decentralization to be applied. As one example, Behrman et al. (2002) stated that both administrative decentralization and fiscal decentralization have to be implemented together in order to achieve effective end results. Moreover, pressures underlying administrative decentralization are closely related to those of fiscal decentralization. Fiscal decentralization entails a transfer of power over the generation and distribution of financial resources to local and regional levels. This signifies that the central government may no longer collect and distribute funding sources. Therefore, local and regional agencies control the collection and distribution of their own financial resources. While there may be multiple, diverse financial restructurings that fall under the general umbrella of fiscal decentralization, it is often an attempt to increase the cost-effectiveness of education and generate greater revenue, such as illustrated in the Brazilian educational reforms in the 1970s and 1980s (Gorostiaga Derqui, 2001).

Given the arguments surrounding fiscal decentralization of greater efficiency and effectiveness (including greater cost-effectiveness), it is noteworthy that fiscal decentralization reforms may not actually lead to an increase in educational spending. Drawing on the example of Brazil, data indicate that overall educational expenditure at the federal level was reduced from $8.1 billion to $3.9 billion between the years of 1988 and 1991, while the portion paid by municipalities rose to $4.7 billion from $3.2 billion (Behrman et al., 2002, p. 31). Still, the federal cut in public expenditure in education resulted in a net $2.7 billion loss. Therefore, even with increased local and regional funding, overall public expenditure in education may decrease, leaving public education systems at the primary and secondary levels without adequate funding. As local and regional levels do not always have sufficient resources to put into schools, goals to enhance social inclusion and equity may be undermined. Privatization may also become a readily advocated and accepted option as educational systems face increased educational demands and local and regional financial resources are strained.

Similar to administrative decentralization, fiscal decentralization appears to be a response to the changing organization of the state. Fiscal decentralization is often advocated in circumstances in which the central state is unable economically to supply adequate public expenditure in education. In this way, a scaled-back role of the central state, in the generation, collection, and distribution of financial resources, transfers the financial responsibility to regional and local levels. However, this does not necessarily signify an increase in local or regional decision-making over the ways in which funding resources are spent, and/or control over policy production. Similar to administrative decentralization, there are typically accountability and transparency strategies in place to audit the ways in which financial resources are allocated. A brief example drawn from the case of fiscal decentralization in the Philippines' education system provides another illustration.

Under the Local Government Code of 1991 in the Philippines, fiscal decentralization was implemented, followed by large increases in local level expenditures on education. Behrman et al. (2002) wrote "local government expenditures on education rose nearly sevenfold—from P0.8 billion in 1991 to P5.7 billion in 1996. This resulted in a large increase in the percentage of public spending on education accounted for by LGUs—from about 2.1 percent in 1990 to 8.3 percent in 1994" (p. 34). However, the authors went on to note that the central government in the Philippines still maintained all governmental responsibilities in education.

In fact, some central governments that employ fiscal decentralization even prohibit local level policy production, in areas of setting standards and/or making decisions over the curriculum (Behrman et al., 2002). Even with increased fiscal responsibilities at local and regional levels, the state maintains an important role in the production of policy, which has particular implications for local and regional decision-making. This appears to be more of an administrative form of decentralization, in which local levels are increasingly responsible for fiscal matters, although they remain steered by the state in matters of decision-making, standard-setting, and financial matters. In fact, in many examples, fiscal responsibilities decentralized to regional and local levels are mandated by central state governments. This leaves regional and local levels to gain little autonomy over educational decision-making matters.

While these three conceptions of decentralization are helpful in framing underlying purposes, meanings, and conditions of educational decentralization, it is important to note that decentralization is above all a dynamic and complex process, and not a static concept (Bray & Mukundan, 2003). It is clear that in the process of educational decentralization, there are multiple pressures, including historic and contextual specificities, which shape the form that decentralization takes. As such, one, two, or all three of the above conceptions of decentralization may be combined in the process of educational decentralization. This will be further exemplified by the case of Spain.

CHAPTER 3

CONSTRUCTING THE NEW SPANISH STATE

The most radical changes are those that have occurred in the settings that were in the past the most marginal to the centers of power.
(Nash, 2001, p. xi)

Drawing from the contemporary debates of globalization, the reformation of the nation state and shifts in educational governance, this chapter focuses specifically on the construction of the new Spanish state in the post-Franco era of democratization. By focusing on the reconstruction of post-Franco Spain and the renewed quest for Catalan autonomy, it puts a "face" on the modern nation state machine, and allows us to be able to trace the pliability and at times even volatile reformation of a nation state in an era of economic, political and cultural globalization. This rebirth of the Spanish state, which is always in a position of incompleteness, sheds light on the new conditions of globalization explored in the previous chapter, including pressures of integration and fragmentation, movement and migration, time/space compression, new forms of educational governance, and new policy actors.

SPANISH DEMOCRATIZATION

Robert Cowen (2003) argued that one can "read the global" through what he has called "transitologies." For Cowen, transitologies are

> the more or less simultaneous collapse and reconstruction of (1) state apparatuses; (b) social and economic stratification systems; and (c) political visions of the future; in which (d) education is given a major symbolic and reconstructionist role in these social processes of destroying the past and redefining the future. (p. 10)

These processes happen roughly in a decade or less and as they occur quickly and suddenly, these moments "reveal to us, behind their drama and their rhetoric, the educational patterns that are ordinarily...difficult to see..." and are "moments of major metamorphosis" (Cowen, p. 11). Post-Franco Spain is one such illustrative example.

Over the past thirty years, Spain's democratization efforts have vastly changed the structure of the Spanish state and brought about a modern mass education system. These efforts came at the end of a 40-year Fascist dictatorship, lasting from 1939 to 1975, with the death of General Francisco Franco. The adoption of the *Constitución Española* (Spanish Constitution) into law in 1978 is regarded as a cornerstone of Spain's democratization efforts and the legal embracing of a democratic organization and set of civic values. Spain's transition into one of the EU's core democracies is often cited as a successful, "miracle model," most recently for Central and Eastern EU countries once behind the Iron Curtain of communism.

Throughout the process of democratization, Spain underwent vast and dramatic transformation and reinvention, including the recognition of 17 autonomous communities (CCAA). The Spanish Constitution recognized the various national communities, particularly Catalonia, the Basque Country, and Galicia, while also simultaneously labeling Spain as a "sole collective entity to have full sovereignty" (Núñez Seixas, 2005, p. 122). The challenge to achieve unification and recognize the diverse needs of the CCAA underlies contemporary political debates, including those surrounding education. However, the challenge of national unity has been a long historical struggle in Spain over hundreds of years.

A detailed historical overview of the long and complex relationship between Spain and Catalonia and their political institutions is well beyond the scope of this book. Nonetheless, it is significant to note that widespread oppression in the name of unity has been well ingrained in Spanish history. As early as the 15th century, Castilian hegemonic forces began to repress communities along what became known as the peripheries of Spain, in which the Castilian language and Spanish nationalism become one in the same. Throughout the 18th and 19th centuries, Spain used the promotion of a national language as means to link citizens together and to enhance political participation. There were periods of political, cultural, and linguistic resurgence and cultural revival. However, these were typically followed by repressive periods of centralization. At the dawn of the 20th century, Spain, much like a pendulum, swung back towards strict, centralized rule.

In the early 20th century, an authoritarian political organization was developed, called the Falange, which was linked to the dictatorship led by Primo de Rivera in the 1930s. During the Civil War, the Falange sided with the Nationalists and became a leading force under Franco. The Falange combined with the Carlist Party and along with General Franco, they became the political organization, *Falange Española Tradicionalista y de las Juntas de Ofensive Nacional-Sindicalista* (FET), which was also called the *Movimiento Nacional* (National Movement) (Muñoz & Marcos, 2005). During this period, an overwhelming suppressive agenda towards cultural and linguistic minorities was invoked, as Franco's social and political vision underpinned the "fortif[ication of] the 'New Spanish State'" (Hanson, 2000, p. 13). The development of a Francoist state had a profound impact on the Spanish educational system, and recent educational reforms over the past three decades

Construction of the Francoist state

At the end of the 1930s, with the Civil War victory of Franco and the nationals, backed by the old aristocracy, upper class, and the Catholic Church, the Francoist regime was established. The central values underpinning the Francoist political project included nationalist rhetoric, little political and cultural freedom, the creation of a strong central state concentrated on the political and military power of one man, "*el generalismo,*" the declaration of the state as officially Catholic, with the Catholic Church having extensive cultural and educational control, a lack of political mobility among citizens, and intellectual and cultural poverty as a result of censure and the exile of many intellectuals (Muñoz & Marcos, 2005, p. 151).

The strong Francoist central state did not necessarily extend into the construction of a public education system. Rather, the public education system became marked by the sheer absence of the state. A clear example is the percentage of Gross National Product (GNP) expended on public education, which in 1975 was 1.78%, as compared to 5.1% European average (this included the USSR) and 4% African average in 1975 (Hanson, 1989a, p. 41). Essentially, under the Francoist regime, public education was used in the building of a Spanish citizenry around nationalism, a centralized military state, and Catholicism, all part and parcel of the overarching aims to establish Spanish unity and uniformity. One of the first actions taken by the Francoist regime was the dismantling of "the flexible, liberalized education system of the democratically elected Second Republic" (Hanson, 2000, p. 13). The Francoist regime then handed educational control over to the Catholic Church, in terms of organization, regulation, and funding.

Although the educational system for Franco and the nationals was considered a core institution in which to interject the central values of the new Francoist state, mass public education was viewed largely as an expenditure rather than an investment in the future of Spain. As such, privatization served as means for the government to cut public expenditure, and a dual system of private and public schools was developed. This fit within Franco's general vision that education should be reserved for society's elite (Hanson, 2000). During the 40-year Francoist dictatorship, the Spanish education system "was characterized by the Church's monopoly...a rigid institutional structure, and by an extreme uniformity and centralization" (Esturla, 2000, p. 322). Private schools, which were run by the Catholic Church, required fees and offered a higher quality education for those who could afford the cost of the fees. Public schools on the other hand, which did not require any fees, were attended by the economically less advantaged and provided a lower quality education.

Historically, the development of a private sector in Spain also played a key role in filling the educational gap left by the absence of the state. Across Spain, the private sector allowed for greater access to educational opportunities, otherwise silenced by the lack of a state-supported public education system for all citizens. As an example, in the autonomous community of Catalonia, the private education sector offered Catalan citizens enhanced educational opportunities. Ultimately, however, the private-public sector divide in education existed as a form of institutionalized inequality. This inequality was inherited by the Spanish educational system in the post-Franco era, as public institutions underwent a process of democratization. This issue is discussed further in chapter 4.

As typical under authoritarian rule, the Francoist regime was largely preoccupied with stability. This is reflected in the highly centralized Spanish educational system. For the masses, education was seen as a vehicle for promoting nationalist rhetoric and Catholic values, as demonstrated in the public school use of a "cultural transmission model based on ideological control rather than instrumental knowledge" (Bonal, 2000, p. 203). In general, textbooks often focused on three main areas: Catholicism, Spanish nationalism, and Franco as *el caudillo* (the maximum leader) (Hanson, 1989a). Franco himself was glorified throughout society and in schools. One textbook read: "Our tranquility and security we owe to Franco. The Caudillo is beloved by all: his name is pronounced lovingly and with blind faith in the destiny of Spain" (Villar, 1984, p. 345-348).

Villar (1984) went on to cite another excerpt from a textbook, which stated that Franco was "elected God as the restorer of Christian civilization, author of peace and well-being, father of his family and father of all Spaniards, model of the Spanish gentleman, and great protector of children and young people" (p. 345-348). Historic images and "supreme symbols of national unity" also were invoked to illicit a national sense of *lo español* (that which is Spanish), such as historical references to Catholicism from the Roman period, the Reconquista, referring to the Christian conquering of the Iberian Peninsula from the Moors and the exile of the Jews, and the Spanish Catholic Monarchs (Muñoz & Marcos, 2005, p. 176; my translation). In addition to textbooks and the promotion of symbolic images, it is reported that over 60,000 teachers between 1936 and 1945 were forcibly reassigned, suspended, or fired, replaced by a member of the Falange (Hanson, 1989b, 2000).

During the years of the Francoist dictatorship, an overwhelming suppressive agenda towards cultural and linguistic minorities was invoked. For Franco and the nationalist movement, expressions of regional nationalism were synonymous with the undermining of the project of Spanish unity and thus, subject to reprimand. Following the Civil War, Franco's position towards Catalonia was one of hostility and resentment, and many leading Catalan figures and intellectuals were forced into exile or executed. Hughes (1993) wrote that "Barcelona ha[d] been the last bastion of resistance to Franco, and the dictator never forgave the city for it" (p. 8). Franco also resented Barcelona because of its open port, which had potential of giving way to "the influence of foreigners, to strange and nonnative ways…[and] offering an ease of entry and exit that a landlocked capital does not" (Hughes, 1993, p. 8-9). In the post-Civil War developments, the diverse communities of Spain were largely treated as occupied territories after the Civil War.

As a result, the language of Catalonia, along with all regional languages in Spain, were silenced and condemned on the street, in print, in schools, in politics, and in communication. Balcells (1996) wrote that the Francoist dictatorship

> was confident that by excluding the Catalan language from the radio, the daily press, the cinema, the schools and, later, from television, it would succeed in cutting off the great majority of the population from the difficult rebirth of Catalan national awareness. (p. 144)

Catalan names used on ships and boats had to be translated to Castilian, beginning in 1945, and Catalan names were banned from civil registries. One account described Franco's declaration of Catalan, the language of Catalonia, as nothing more than "la lengua de perros," ("the tongue of dogs"), as Franco encouraged

Barcelona police to reprimand the use of Catalan, in which Catalan-speakers were ordered "Habla Cristiano!" "Speak Christian!" invoking once again a Castilian identity synonymous with Christianity (Grant, 1988, p. 157). This suppressive agenda continued even as Spain opened its borders and experienced economic growth in the latter half of the Francoist dictatorship.

Democratization/Europeanization of the Spanish State

Spain's transition into a social democratic state and the democratization of public institutions inherited from the Francoist era seem to be widely influenced by Spain's engagement with both European and global pressures (Engel, 2007b). First, Spain's dramatic transformation over the past 30 years is largely due to the opening up of the Spanish market in the early 1960s to international competition and "social modernization following the introduction of Fordism" (Holman, 1996, p. 29). While the first half of the Francoist years can be characterized as highly centralized, the latter half is known for massive economic growth due to market liberalization, industrialization, and the development of its tourist industry (Guillén & Álvarez, 2001; MacLennan, 2000). The opening of the Spanish market was paired with the embracing of "a new political discourse based on 'democracy' and modernization" on the part of Spanish citizens, reflecting global and European influences (Bonal, 2000, p. 203).

While the transition to democracy was eased given the societal embrace of discourses of democratization, the reform of Spanish public institutions, including education, posed a formidable challenge. As Torres and Piña (2004) pointed out:

in the 1970s, in comparison with other OECD countries, Spain had a small and unbalanced public sector, with important deficiencies in infrastructures and limited activities in the fields of the redistribution of wealth, welfare, health, education, social and cultural services. (p. 447)

In the beginning of the transition, Spain's difficulty in reforming the educational sector to meet policy goals of equity and equality of educational access was similar to the challenges many Western countries encountered given the global economic crisis of the mid-1970s. Guillén and Álvarez (2001) argued that the 1970s oil crisis halted Spanish economic growth and made implementation of social policies and an overhaul of public institutions inherited from the Francoist era difficult, given the lack of state funding. In the late 1970s, Spain's dependence on oil, which was steadily rising in cost, brought about a number of political and economic challenges. In 1977, the inflation of Spain was 24.5%, while unemployment grew from "6 per cent of the active population in 1977 to 17 per cent in 1981" (Heywood, 1995, p. 95). This posed many issues for the reform of the public sector reform and the consolidation of democracy in Spain. After winning the 1982 election, the Spanish Socialist Worker's Party's (*Partido Socialista Obrero Español*, PSOE) efforts included a program, which aimed to reinforce administrative efficiency across the state (Heywood, 1995). It also resulted in a shift in policy from "attention to equity in social policy…in favour of a search for efficiency" (Guillén & Álvarez, 2001, p. 115). This shift is in part a consequence of the Spanish state looking towards the European Community (EC) and OECD countries as models for economic growth, social stability, and public policy.

During the 1980s, the overarching goal of the PSOE was the modernization of Spain in order to gain accession to the EC. As Jones (2000) pointed out, "EC accession was of fundamental importance for the newly established democracy" (p. 9). In the 1970s and 1980s, "Becoming Europeans" was an expression used in Spanish political rhetoric as it "implied economic growth, and an improvement of social policy along the lines of the social democratic, Scandinavian systems" (Guillén & Álvarez, 2001, p. 113). In the latter half of the Francoist years and in particular, during Spain's transition to democratization, Europe was a model for economic prosperity, advancement in social policy, and modernization. In other words, in the development of the Spanish state during the transition period, there was a dominant "myth of Europe, which epitomized everything that was modern" (Farrell, 2005, p. 215). The diverse communities of Spain also characterized Europe in a similar fashion. For example, in Catalonia, "joining European 'high civility' and becoming European citizens were objectives for Catalonia to aspire to in order to become a modern and democratic society" (Giordano & Roller, 2002, p. 104). Spain's first application for EU membership was in 1977 and negotiations for accession began in 1979. These negotiations lasted seven years and centered on Spain's adaptation to the EC's common agricultural policy and the acclimatization of Spain's economy.

Ultimately, Spain's 1986 accession to the EC allowed for Spain to engage directly in vigorous pursuit of policies aligned with European interests. EC membership also provided Spain with a strong boost economically in order to reform public policy and build the public infrastructure necessary for a democratized Spain (Gillespie, 2000). During this period, efficiency was emphasized, as evident in the implementation of policies aligned with the NPM doctrine, which was rigorously introduced in order to advance the Spanish system of public administration (Torres & Piña, 2004). However, these new policy directions also brought about a new set of challenges, particularly in light of Spain's recent transition to democracy. Heywood (1995) argued "the Socialist government was faced with the daunting challenge of reconciling the promotion of social justice with competitive expansion in order to prepare Spain for entry to the EC" (p. 220). Citizens became increasingly frustrated with the Socialist Party's leader, Felipe González, and what they viewed as a lack of social policy development in Spain. The policy reform efforts under the leadership of González have been referred to not as socialist, but as neoliberal, in which he has often been aligned with Reagan and Thatcher.

Pedro Almodóvar's (1996) film, *La Flor de Mi Secreto* (The Flower of My Secret) offered a colorful depiction of citizen protests against González and the Socialist Party's policies and their vision of a Europeanized Spain. Almodóvar's (1996) work also underlined debates between conceptions of old, traditional Spanish values and new values of Europeanization. The film's central protagonist, Leo, travels a path of confusion over the difficulty maintaining her relationship with her Europeanized husband, Felipe. Felipe has taken a military position with the EU in Brussels as part of the NATO peacekeeping mission in Bosnia. In the process of a failed marriage, Leo meets and befriends Ángel, who brings Leo back to her roots in what is depicted as the beautiful and tranquil traditional Spanish *pueblo*.

Throughout the film, much like the life of Leo, Spain appears to be depicted as if it is on a tension-filled journey (Engel, 2007b). On the journey, Spain is confronted with contrasting notions of constructed nationalist traditionalism and the notion of Europe as a sense of freedom and the path forward; although Almodóvar seems to be arguing that it may be a path that will ultimately lead to a hollowing out of the Spanish state, making Spain forgetful of its own national identity and history. In one scene, Leo's mother compliments Ángel on his healthy physique, stating, "My Leo used to be healthy too, she was a chubby little girl, like you, Ángel, until she started to diet." The fleshy build of Ángel sharply contrasts with the lean, stern image of Leo's husband in Brussels and the current frail state of Leo.

Examining the character of Leo in this light, as she confronts the remains of her broken marriage to her husband, while being helped back to life by Ángel, a plump, jolly, healthy Spaniard, who takes her back to the traditions of the *pueblo*, Almodóvar appeared to be urging Spain to turn back towards the former richness of its own traditions in order to revive itself, rather than towards European modernization. These dual visions of Spain also play out in the development of education policy in what Núñez Seixas (2005) has called "national-catholic nostalgia" on the one hand versus "EU idealism" on the other. Much of this literature has upheld the nation state-Europe dualities, in which Europe and Spain are pitted against one another in a "zero-sum game" (Dale, 2005). Through the 1990s and the current decade's reform movements in Spain, these dualities continue to be utilized to frame the regeneration of the Spanish state, especially in regard to education policy formation.

MODERN MASS EDUCATION IN SPAIN

Before the death of Franco in 1975, the first Spanish law of education was passed, representing one of the final laws passed during the dictatorship. Since the Spanish law of education in 1970, many reform efforts and debates have followed. An overview of educational legislation frames these debates and offers a dynamic notion of the ways in which policy is produced within particular social, political, cultural, and economic contexts. For analytical purposes, I draw on Bonal and Rambla's (1996) and Bonal's (1998, 2000) discussion of Spanish education policy production during the period of democratization, beginning as early as 1970. I also utilize excerpts of the actual educational legislation from the period of 1970 to 2006.

The 1970 General Law of Education (*Ley General de Educación*-LGE) represented the first major educational act since 1857. The law emphasized equality of educational opportunity and the benefits of a meritocracy, which was seen as the first stage in achieving a modern capitalist state and society. Bonal (2000) pointed out that the "rhetoric [of meritocracy and equality] and the European expansion of education in the sixties stimulated a rise in educational expectations and, therefore, generated pressures to expand the education system" (p. 203). It is out of the 1970 legislation that a system of modern mass education in Spain was born. One major mandate of the LGE was obligatory school attendance for all citizens under the age of 14. This brought about a significant increase in educational enrollment patterns in Spain. Hanson (2000) noted that the number of public schools increased from 1,100 in 1975 to approximately 3,000 in 1995 and compared with the 44% of school attendance of 15 year olds in 1975, approximately 100% of 15 year olds were enrolled in 1995.

The period from 1978 to 1982 is marked by the democratization of educational access in the form of free public education and the construction of schools. The major education act of 1980 was entitled the Organic Law of the Statute of Scholastic Centers (*Ley Orgánica del Estatuto de Centros Escolares*-LOECE), which served as a major political conflict between the right and the left (Bonal, 2000). The right (represented by the UCD-Democratic Center Union) established the 1980 law to ensure "conditions for free school choice and attempted to limit the participation of the educational community by submitting it to the will of the school proprietor" (Bonal, 2000, p. 204). This was vehemently opposed by the left, which did not support the free choice ideology and mapped greater educational responsibility onto the state. This debate continued with the election of the PSOE in 1982, allowing for the left's opposition to the existing legislation to materialize in the abolishment of the 1980 law (Bonal, 2000). The initial years of the Socialist Party's term in the 1980s was marked by attempts to modernize the education system in accordance with the development of European standards of education. It largely included policies seeking to improve public education both in its "extension and organization" (Bonal, 1998, p. 154; my translation).

Substituting for the 1980 law, the 1985 Regulatory Organic Law of the Right to Education (*Ley Orgánica del Derecho a la Educación*-LODE*)* was passed, which decentralized educational responsibility, signifying a different role of the state with respect to educational governance, and brought about important structural developments (Edge, 2000). As the LODE emphasized the importance of decentralization to democratization, there was recognition of the need for "a system of participation where all sectors of society have the right to decide about issues of organization, pedagogy, and educational finance" (Hanson, 2000, p. 46). It was this legislation (and that of the early 1990s) that established a multilevel system of educational governance "with the creation of school councils in which parents were represented, and trends towards stronger management and steering at school level" (Pereyra, 2002, p. 668). Multiple agencies and councils at various local and regional levels were established to create a decentralized system.

As a result, parents, teachers, unions, students, and local level communities could be represented in the educational system. Edge (2000) discussed the development of the State School Council (*Consejo Escolar del Estado*-CEE), as an 80 member national advisory body representing teachers, parents, unions, administrators, and scholars. The main responsibilities of the State School Council have been to submit proposals for educational change. The Conference of Education Counselors also was established, which brought together the Ministry of Education and Science (MEC), the Chief Education Officers (CEOs) of all CCAA systems, the *Consejos Escolares del Centro* (Education Council), and *Consejos Escolares* (Local School Councils).

Following the 1985 reform were two policy documents: *Proyecto para la Reforma de la Enseñanza* (debated in 1987 and completed in 1988) and *El Libro Blanco para la Reforma del Sistema Educativo* (1989). These two reports detailed the underlying debates of educational reform during this period, indicating particular educational actors, central questions, problems, and necessary changes to make in order to improve the Spanish educational system. These reports formed the backbone of the 1990 Organic Law on the General Organization of the Educational System (LOGSE). Fierro (1994) developed a detailed overview of the debates leading up to and surrounding the enactment of the LOGSE. In essence, this law represented a major effort to overhaul the Spanish educational system. The main aspects of reform included basic education as compulsory and free, extended to the age of 16, the expansion of vocational education to all students, reduction of educational inequity, and mandated improvements in the quality of teaching (Fierro, 1994; Petrongolo & San Segundo, 2002). New mandates also included a focus on excellence in all institutions of education, equality of educational opportunities, and "an explicit objective to not lose ground in the process of European convergence" (Bonal, 1998, p. 156, my translation).

In addition, under OECD directives and policy influences generated from other IOs, Spanish education policy began to reflect global and EU pressures. One example is the importance of vocational education, primarily through the pursuit of Leonardo da Vinci grants, which are part of a EU program aimed to aid in the development of lifelong learning through vocational training. Although the LOGSE aimed to make large strides in the improvement of educational access and the promotion of equal educational opportunities, Teasley (2004) argued that the legislation continued the exclusion of immigrant and Romani students. This was the result of its definition of

> the average student primarily through three, key, cultural, political and economic spaces: the *nation-state*, through the "citizen" figure; the *Autonomous Community*, in recognition of regional cultural diversity; and *Europe*, as *the* international community *par excellence* for the discourse on progress in the law. (Teasley, 2004, p. 255, author's italics)

This definition of the average student in the LOGSE excluded immigrant and Romani students, even within discussions of greater educational access and equality to educational opportunities.

The PSOE also enacted the Organic Law on Participation, Assessment and Governance of Institutions of Education (*Ley Orgánica de Participación, Evaluación y Gobierno de los Centros Educativos*-LOPEG). This 1995 law aimed to regulate the evaluation of educational institutions. As part of the move towards excellence and quality assurance, there were also developments in educational investigation, inspection, and evaluation (MEC, 1999). While implementation of the 1990 LOPEG was still underway, the Popular Party (*Partido Popular*, PP) won the 1996 elections over the PSOE. In 1996, PP took on the reformation of the public sector with neoliberal ideologies of privatization, market liberalization, and an increase in quality and efficiency, leading to a decrease in attention given to equality and social inclusion. After proposing its initial legislation without majority support, the PP was able to enact the Organic Law on Quality in Education (*Ley Orgánica de Calidad de la Educación*-LOCE) (MEC, 2002).

One of the most debated aspects of the LOCE was the allowance of students to repeat grade levels. According to Rafael Artacho López (2006) the LOCE aimed to improve the rates of adolescent school drop out through the creation of a culture of effort, an exterior system of evaluation and control over educational centers, and increasing the prestige surrounding the social role of school and professors in society. Additionally, Calero (2005) argued that LOCE introduced "tracks at the age between 15 and 16 years...with the object of providing greater flexibility, adapted to individual needs" (p. 14). Opponents to the law saw these efforts as an overemphasis on market efficiency and training, rather than a substantial effort towards meeting the goals of education to facilitate greater equity and social inclusion.

Critics also argued that the LOCE's establishment of tracking due to the diversity of Spanish pupils was a masked effort of increasing system efficiency through the division of students between upper (more academic) and lower (more vocational) tracks. With implementation of the 2002 law just barely off the ground (implementation began in 2003), new leadership of the Socialist Party in Spain in 2004 introduced a series of policy reforms. Under the new direction of José Luis Rodríguez Zapatero, President of the Socialist Party, a new educational bill was proposed. The bill was heavily publicized with debates mainly over the teaching of religion. In May 2006, the new educational legislation was passed, entitled the Organic Law of Education (*Ley Orgánica de Educación*-LOE). The LOE will be discussed at greater length in the following chapter.

In the several decades of dynamic political shifts and rapid policy production, it is noteworthy that processes of democratization in Spain have not been free of conflict. Whereas the Spanish Constitution was fashioned as a guiding model for the consolidation of democratic values and the achievement of a decentralized, yet unified nation state system in politics and public policy-making, there have been many uncertainties. As the mass modern educational system has developed in the post-Franco period in Spain, it has been marked by the nature of the relationship between the central Spanish state and the regions. The following section explores the case of Catalonia, including a brief overview of its history, cultural and linguistic roots, and the trends that have shaped this dynamic space, ranging from immigration to the struggle for greater autonomy through cultural and linguistic identity politics.

CATALUNYA

Spain is a thing made of Castile.
(José Ortega y Gasset)

Identities are never unified...and increasingly fragmented and fractured; never singular but multiply constructed across different, often intersecting and antagonistic discourses, practices, and positions.
(Hall & duGay, 1996, p. 4)

Barcelona, the capital of Catalonia, is in many ways a busy, cosmopolitan intersection of rapid movement and noisy coexistence, not always a peaceful one, of individuals from around the world. Largely the result of industrialization and rapid economic growth in Catalonia, Barcelona was a destination of migration for many Spaniards from other, less developed parts of Spain in the 20th century, and more recently, immigrants from North Africa and Latin America. As Marian Hens (2007) reported, "since 2000, Spain has absorbed around four million immigrants. Just less than a quarter have settled in prosperous Catalonia" (para. 4).

This is remarkable given that not long ago, Spain was a source of many immigrant workers seeking employment in other European countries, and it now attracts a large number of immigrant workers from abroad. Catalonia's history of international commerce, the millions of tourists and its subsistence as a popular study abroad location for students around the world add to Barcelona's existence as a global city. In Barcelona, a space of multidimensional and multicultural overlap, there is an awareness of the cultural and political landscape of Catalonia etched out over many centuries. In William Faulkner's well-known expression, "the past is not dead. It's not even past."

In light of the developing democratic state of Spain, this chapter provides a historical backdrop to the Catalan nation and its quest for greater autonomy. It is worth noting that this chapter paints broad brushstrokes across centuries of conflict and tendencies of centralization and decentralization, and in doing so, risks oversimplification of these historical processes. Nonetheless, it is helpful to address major events and historical periods to provide a backdrop for a case study of education policy in Spain and Catalonia. Second, a historical perspective is necessary because of the complexity involved in conceptions of the nation, the state, and particularly, notions of the nation state that have existed across centuries. I want to argue specifically that these concepts must not be seen as fixed, neutral entities. Building from the discussion in the previous chapter, these concepts are rooted in particular histories, and are socially constructed and politically produced. This is particularly evident in the case of Catalonia.

History of Catalonia

Catalonia has the status of one of the historical nations in the establishment of the State of Autonomies in Spain. It is located in the northeastern region (just slightly larger than Belgium) of the Iberian Peninsula, bordering the Mediterranean Sea, France, Andorra, Aragon, and Valencia. Catalonia is made up of four provinces: Barcelona (its capital), Gerona, Leida, and Tarragona. According to the Catalan Institute of Statistics, Catalonia has the second largest population out of the 17 CCAA in Spain (the largest is Andalusia), with over 7 million inhabitants reported in a 2008 census. The population of Catalonia makes up roughly 16% of the total population of Spain. While discussed in detail in this section, it is noteworthy that Catalan cultural and linguistic identity is not limited to the territory of Catalonia described here. Balcells (2006) pointed out

> Catalan identity is not confined to Catalonia proper since the Catalan language is spoken in a much larger area inhabited by a total of 11 million people and comprising Catalonia itself, the Kingdom of Valencia, the Balearic Islands, the Principality of Andorra, and the Catalan regions which were annexed to France in 1659. (p. 1)

As early as the 9th century, Catalonia emerged as an independent entity, with self-governing political institutions and laws (Guibernau, 1999). Politically, Catalonia's origins are linked to feudal counties in the northern territories of the Iberian Peninsula during the Islamic conquest.

The Iberian Peninsula's history consists of subsequent invasions, a consequence of its geographical location. In 711, Muslim forces invaded the Iberian Peninsula, and the parts of the Iberian Peninsula ruled by Muslims became known by the Arabic name, Al-Andalus. Al-Andalus was separated from the Frankish kingdom by the Hispanic March (*Marca Hispánica*), which existed just south of the Pyrenees Mountains. The area north of the Hispanic March was "a territory divided into nine earldoms, all of which enjoyed equal status" (Balcells, 1996, p. 2). These areas existed as "a thoroughfare, an area where contacts could take place between Al-Andalus and the Christian western world," which was quite different from other Christian territories in the Pyrenees that were isolated from both Al-Andalus and Carolingian Europe (Balcells, 1996, p. 2). In the development of the Carolingian Empire, the Frankish rule placed substantial power in the hands of local elites, eventually leading to an independent House of Barcelona in the 9th century, with the last Count of Barcelona, Guifré el Pilós (Wilfred the Hairy), "receiv[ing] his commission from the Frankish king" (Guibernau, 1999, p. 39). Balcells (1996) wrote that

> owing to the decline of the power of the monarchy in France, the eastern earldoms became hereditary from the time of the Count Wilfred the Hairy who, in 878, was able to unite under his rule the earldoms of Barcelona, Girona, Osona, Urgell, and Cerdanya. (p. 3)

As the power of the House of Barcelona grew in the 11th and 12th centuries, this area became known as Catalonia, according to the first documents found from this time that recorded inhabitants of this territory by the term "Catalan" (Balcells, 1996). During the 12th century, Catalonia was united with the Kingdom of Aragon.

In 1137, Catalonia and Aragon formed a union under Ramon Berenguer IV, although each remained politically separate, with independent governing institutions. In 1359, the Deputation of the General (*Diputació del General*) was made official as one of the first parliaments in Europe. In 1403, the *Palau de la Generalitat* was constructed. This building still exists today as one of the few medieval European buildings that continue to house its original and intended institution. This building also exists as a valuable symbol of Catalan democracy, and the sustenance of Catalan institutions throughout centuries of conflict.

In the centuries that followed the union of Catalonia and Aragon, Catalonia's commerce and coastal trade was massively expanded, lending to the construction of "a powerful Mediterranean empire of a primarily commercial character... [including] Valencia, Majorca, Sardinia, Corsica, Sicily, Naples, Athens and Neopatria, as well as French territories beyond the Pyrenees particularly Roussillon and Cerdagne" (Guibernau, 1999, p. 39). As Jaume I conquered these territories, the political and economic strength of Catalonia grew rapidly throughout the 13th and 14th centuries. In the rest of the Iberian Peninsula, the Christian frontier slowly moved southward, in which the *Reconquista* was aimed at reviving the power of the Christian rule over the Iberian Peninsula. The 1400s brought many changes to the Iberian Peninsula, shaping what we know today as Spain and Catalonia.

During this period, the Catholic Kings, represented by the union of Ferdinand of Aragon and Isabella of Castile, joined together the rule of Castile with the Crown of Aragon (consisting of Catalonia, Valencia, and Aragon) in 1479 (Guibernau, 1999). It was the marriage of two very distinct political institutions, and Catalonia and Aragon were able to preserve each of their respective sovereign institutions of law, currency, and tax collection. The Iberian Peninsula, however, was drastically changed by this union, with the long rule of the Muslims coming to a close with their expulsion in 1492 by the Catholic Kings. During the same year, after a tumultuous history, Jews also were expelled. Upon the death of Ferdinand, the position of Castile gradually changed, with more attention given to the formation of a "powerful absolutist state" regulated by Castile (Guibernau, 1999, p. 40).

Rule over the Iberian Peninsula also changed by the increased power bestowed in chief ministers appointed by the successor Kings of Castile. The Count-Duke of Olivares was appointed by King Felipe IV in 1621, and ruled over Spain's foreign policy for the next 22 years. During this period, tensions grew between Catalonia and Castile. As Castile grew increasingly poor due in part to the number of wars Spain engaged in the 1600s, it began to seek financial income from the different kingdoms through increasingly centralist policies. As a result of the build-up of these tensions, farmers of Catalonia revolted in 1640, known as the War of the Harvesters (also as the Revolt of the Reapers).

In 1700, the last of the Habsburg Kings, Charles II, died and left no heir to the throne. This ended the Habsburg dynasty in Spain. As a successor, Charles II named Philippe of Bourbon, Duke of Anjou, who was the grandson of King Louis XIV of France. As an alternative successor, he named a family member from the Austrian side of the Habsburgs. Philippe of Bourbon became known as Felipe V and he was named the next King of Spain. Consequently, European countries were left divided, with England, the Netherlands, and Austria opposing the growing power of King Louis XIV. This led to one of the most significant events in the history of Catalonia: the War of the Spanish Succession of 1701 to 1714. Ultimately, Felipe V was named the King of Spain by the 1713 Treaty of Utrecht, which began the dynasty of the Bourbons in Spain. The current King of Spain, Juan Carlos I of Spain continues this dynasty today.

For Catalonia, the War of the Spanish Succession put an end to their independence. As other European nations took sides over the next Spanish throne in the dawn of the 18th century, Catalonia sided against Felipe V and backed the succession of the Austrian Habsburgs. At the end of the war, Catalonia "was left alone to face the might of the Franco-Spanish armies" (Guibernau, 1999, p. 40). On September 11, 1714, Catalonia finally surrendered in Barcelona to the Franco-Spanish armies, followed by Felipe V's 1716 *Decreto de Nueva Planta*, a new plan that centralized the government of Catalonia under the rule of Castile. Consequently, all Catalan institutions (Council of One Hundred, Diputació, and the Generalitat) were dismantled.

As Castile faced serious bankruptcy issues, Catalonia was heavily taxed, so much so that "the Spanish monarchy wiped out its financial deficit through the fiscal exploitation of the countries of the former Crown of Aragon" (Balcells, 1996, p. 16). Although appeals continued to be made to the parliament for Catalonia's political autonomy to be reinstated, Catalonia remained under the authority of the Spanish monarchy, which looked towards absolutist France as a model. This also included the ban on public usage of the Catalan language. Guibernau (1999) stated that "Catalan was forbidden and Castilian (Spanish) was proclaimed as the official language" (p. 40-41). However, it was not until the 19th century that Castilian Spanish was enforced in education and public documents (Balcells, 1996).

As a result of Catalonia's absorption under centralist power in a state constructed by Castile, its independence disappeared. As Spain faced off with France in the early 1800s, Catalonia was caught between "two centralist régimes [Spain and Napoleanic France] with assimilatory intentions and in such circumstances the victory of the weaker of the two, Spain, seemed for the Catalans the lesser of two evils" (Balcells, 1996, p. 17). Moreover, Catalonia's position is often interpreted during this period as "a sign of consolidated Spanish nationalism" (Balcells, 1996, p. 17). However, Balcells (1996) noted that Catalonia's position, in particular the Junta de Cataluña, was an act in the name of Catalan self-government, which actually provided Spain a model of a "liberal-type political Constitution," and would later "constitute a precedent for the future Catalan federalist movement" (p. 17). A century after the War of Succession, Spain's empire rapidly declined, which historians have attributed to Spain not becoming swept up in Enlightenment ideas like the rest of Europe, and the failure of the Spanish economy to industrialize at a comparable rate with Germany, Britain, and France. The decline also has been linked to Spain's military defeat and loss of its American empire.

Unlike in the rest of Spain, an industrial revolution did take place in Catalonia. Although there were a number of deficiencies in Catalan industrialization, the Catalan economy was rapidly changed in the 19th century, resulting in the emergence of a Catalan bourgeoisie class. Also during the 19th century, cultural movements emerged through Europe that challenged the hegemonic practices of the nation state construction. I outline these movements below in relation to claims for Catalan nationhood. Here, I want to point out in this historical context that these movements helped create a political environment that aided the emergence of the democratic, however short lived First Spanish Republic, and the materialization of the Second Spanish Republic (Balcells, 1996).

In the early 1900s, the Catalan nationalist movement helped pave the way for the development of the Catalan Mancomunitat, a federation of four Catalan provincial councils established in 1914. Its role did not extend beyond administrative functions and ultimately, "without autonomy, the Mancomunitat could be, in the long run, nothing more than an unsuccessful attempt at establishing a fully Catalan government or 'Generalitat'" (Balcells, 1996, p. 70). Nonetheless, "its very existence marked for the first time recognition of the distinct personality of Catalonia," since 1714 (Balcells, 1996, p. 69). The groundwork laid by the Mancomunitat also allowed for the Generalitat, when it was reinstated during the Second Spanish Republic, to assume many of these Mancomunitat projects, one of which was education.

Under the Mancomunitat, education was advanced as part of the Catalan nationalist movement. The Mancomunitat launched a project to develop Catalan schools, which aimed to "overcome illiteracy and low levels of culture and vocational training; and it meant introducing European pedagogical methods" (Balcells, 1996, p. 70). As part of this educational project, several vocational and post-secondary schools were constructed. These projects were halted by the dictatorship of General Primo de Rivera, with the coup in 1923. During Primo de Rivera's dictatorship (1923-1930), "decrees were promulgated prohibiting the public use of the Catalan language and the exhibition of the Catalan flag in public corporations, dissolving all municipal councils, and closing down…one hundred and forty-nine nationalist organizations" (Balcells, 1996, p. 83). This was followed by the Second Spanish Republic.

Although brief, the Second Spanish Republic is of great importance to understanding the current system of decentralization in Spain. The democratically-elected Second Spanish Republic lasted from 1931 to 1936, followed by the Spanish Civil War of 1936-1939. During the Second Republic, Catalonia and the Basque Country were formally recognized. For example, the Statute of Autonomy in Catalonia was established in 1932, the Statute of Autonomy of the Basque Country was founded in 1936, and the Statute of Autonomy of Galicia was developed although never fully brought to fruition during the Second Republic. The 1931 declaration of a Catalan Republic was the first step towards Catalan self-government. However, Francesc Macià (leader in establishing the Catalan State in 1922) "renounced the Catalan Republic in exchange for a regional government which adopted the historic name of 'the Generalitat'" (Balcells, 1996, p. 94). A draft of Catalonia's Statute of Autonomy was drawn up and passed by a popular vote in 1931, with 99% of voters approving the draft (Balcells, 1996). The Statute outlined the status of the Catalan language as co-official with Castilian Spanish, provided the Generalitat with greater legislative power over administrative and judicial issues in Catalonia, and outlined the relationship between Catalonia and Spain, including issues over taxation and administration.

In order for the final version of Catalonia's Statute of Autonomy to become official, it had to be passed by the Spanish Courts, in which the percentage of Catalan members was very small. In these debates, Balcells (1996) pointed out that the two major areas that were ultimately cut out of the 1930s draft Statute of Autonomy were issues of finance and education. In education, although the draft Statute approved by Catalan people included the "transfer of the entire education system in Catalonia to the Generalitat. Under [the draft Statute] the teaching of Spanish would have been obligatory in all schools, but the language of instruction was to be Catalan" (Balcells, 1996, p. 98). However, in the Statute that was approved by the Spanish Courts in 1932, education was to remain under the control of the Spanish state. This final Statute of Autonomy of 1932 was ultimately eliminated after the Civil War victory of Franco's regime in 1939, along with the Generalitat and all institutions of Catalan self-government in the name of Spanish national unity.

CLAIMS OF CATALAN NATIONHOOD

Often, claims of nationhood encompass three main elements, including language, culture, and characteristics related to a collective social imaginary (Taylor, 2002). Taylor (2002) argued that a social imaginary includes

the ways in which people imagine their social existence, how they fit together with others, how things go on between them and their fellows, the expectations that are normally met, and the deeper normative notions and images that underlie these expectations. (p. 106)

This is comprised of historical traditions, national symbols, such as an anthem, heroes, a flag, and celebrations of independence, myths, and legends. Elements of all three characteristics are embedded in Catalan history, and are entangled in very complex ways. In Catalonia, language is an important expression of cultural, political, and social identity. Catalan is the language of Catalonia, with over 11 million speakers. The official languages in Catalonia are Catalan and Castilian Spanish, and in the Val d'Aran in Catalonia, Aranese also is included as an official language.

However, Catalan is not exclusively spoken in Catalonia. It is also spoken in Valencia (known as Valencian), the Balearic Islands, and southern France. Historically speaking, in *Els Paisos Catalans* (The Catalan Countries), the linguistic heritage of Catalan is considered by linguists to be a Romance language. Contrary to beliefs that Catalonia derived from or is a mix of French and Spanish, which suggests particular power relations between Catalonia, Spain, and France, Catalan is derived from Latin. This is a significant distinction, as Catalan was developed in the period of other romance languages and therefore, offers a historically rich linguistic claim of Catalan nationhood.

The movement of linguistic normalization has been an important process in Catalan nationhood. The movement includes attempts to normalize the Catalan language, particularly in education, through the linguistic normalization laws

(Generalitat de Catalunya, 1983, 1998). In present day, business and correspondence in Catalonia's government is largely carried out in Catalan, and all businesses are required to print and exhibit all information in Catalan. Sanctions have been issued by the Catalan Agency of Consumption for businesses that do not comply with exhibiting all information in Catalan. However, tensions surround issues of Catalan autonomy, language, identity and nationhood, with the influx of Castilian Spanish-speaking immigrants from Latin America. As the Catalan language represents national heritage and the maintenance of an identity autonomous from Castilian Spain, the second and third generational Spanish-speaking migrants from other parts of Spain in the 20th century and the new waves of immigrants have lead to a perceived threat of non-European citizens to a Catalan national identity (Engel & Ortloff, 2009).

Historically, Catalan nationalist expressions have been abundant throughout art and literature. While it is impossible to illustrate the rich history of Catalan cultural expressions, I will nonetheless touch on a number of key figures, which provide a historical backdrop to assertions of Catalan nationhood. During the cultural movements of the *Renaixanca* and *Modernisme* in Catalonia, there were widespread attempts to renew and revive Catalan nationalism. For example, Catalan was rejuvenated in literary movements, which is evident in the 1860s, with the attention given to the writing of literature in Catalan. Key individuals in the Catalan nationalist movement include for example, the 1832 poem by Bonaventura Carles Aribau i Farriols, entitled, *Oda a La Pàtria* (Ode to the Fatherland), the development of the Catalan modern novels by Narcís Oller, and Frederic Soler's *Sainets* (short plays). Two groups of intellectuals and writers of Spain, known respectively as the '98 and '14 Generations largely criticized "the essence of everything that is Spanish" and took a critical position towards the forging of Spanish nationalism (Muñoz & Marcos, 2005, p. 168; my translation). José Ortega y Gasset's famous saying, "Spain is a thing made of Castile," illustrated the pessimism felt towards the imagined construction of the Spanish national identity projected out of Castile.

These literary movements helped spark cultural and linguistic revival movements in the Basque Country and Catalonia, and inspired the political movement of independence from oppressive national governments. The Catalan poet, Joan Maragall, inscribed this movement in *Oda a l'Espanya* (1900),

Where are you, Spain?—nowhere in sight.

Don't you hear my resounding voice?

Don't you understand this language, speaking to you between risks?

Have you left off listening to your sons?

Farewell, Spain!

(as cited in Hughes, 1993)

Famous Catalan artists, such as Gaudí, Rusinyol, and Casas were also important in terms of illustrating and capturing moments of Catalan cultural expression and a Catalan identity, and as such, supported claims of Catalan nationhood.

Additionally, in the 20th century, the *Institut d' Estudis Catalans* (Institute of Catalan Studies) was constructed. Of the many purposes of the Institute were explorations into the particular history of Catalonia (including historical analyses of pre-1714), archeological work exploring roots of Greco-Roman traditions of Catalonia, literature to promote and normalize the Catalan language, and law. In consideration of the Catalan language, the University of Pompeu Fabra, located in Barcelona, was the first institution to standardize the Catalan language, as prior to this point, no texts had been published on Catalan grammar, spelling, syntax, or semantics. In the early 20th century, for example, *Orthographic Rules* of 1913 and *Catalan Grammar* of 1918 were developed to create a standardized Catalan language. These texts mark the importance of language as a central part of the political, social, and cultural campaign underlying the movement of Catalan nationalism. Even as written use of the Catalan language was outlawed during the Francoist dictatorship, periodicals and books continued to be published in exile. Balcells (1996) wrote that 650 books and 180 periodicals were published in Catalan in exile between 1939 and 1975 (p. 143). Balcells (1996) went on to describe the clandestine poetry readings in Catalan that were held around Catalonia, illustrating the ways in which the Catalan language was sustained during the Francoist dictatorship.

Returning back to Taylor (2002), a collective social imaginary has been constructed in Catalonia through myths, stories, and legends, which invoke various symbols of Catalan nationalism. One particular example is the legend of Wilfred the Hairy, the ruler of the Catalan countries in the late-800s. The legend holds that in battle, Wilfred the Hairy was fighting against the Moors, while also simultaneously fighting for the Catalan counties. Up until this point, the legend holds that the Catalan nation possessed no particular sign, symbol, or code of arms. At the time of his death during battle, as the legend describes, Wilfred the Hairy held a golden shield. The fingers of his murderer were dipped in Wilfred's blood and dragged across the shield, forming four red stripes across the golden shield. This legend marks the history of the first Catalan flag, the Senyera (which has been found to be one of the oldest flags used in Europe) and code of arms, which are now significant symbols marking the Catalan nation.

The Catalan anthem, *Els Segadors* is another example of a symbol, used to support the notion of collectivity among Catalan people. The anthem was born during the bloody War of the Harvesters in the 17th century. It now represents what is argued to be the first time that Catalonia fought for its independence. As described earlier, September 11, 1714 marked the loss of Catalan independence to Castile. This date remains the Catalan national day of independence, not as a day that independence was won, but celebrated in the spirit of reviving Catalan independence in the future. The Catalan flag, anthem, and Independence Day all illustrate collective symbols for the Catalan citizenry, used to support claims of Catalonia as a nation.

Political claims of Catalan nationalism are long-standing and rooted in these intellectual and artistic movements. After the loss of political power in 1714, the *Noucentisme* movement of the early 20th century illustrates a movement of normalizing, institutionalizing, and standardizing key aspects of Catalan culture, in order to support Catalan nationalism. *Noucentisme* was coined by Eugeni d'Ors, an intellectual, who was eventually expelled from Catalan politics and was an intellectual of the extreme right during the Spanish Civil War. In 1892, an important political action was undertaken in order to regain political power. A draft of a Catalan document, known as *Bases de Manresa* was constructed and negotiated, indicating the kinds of freedoms and political powers that Catalonia aimed to revive. The political document included Catalan as the official language of Catalonia, the establishment of the *Catalan Corts*, and autonomous control over public services and resources, among other key aspects. The document's primary objective was sovereignty for Catalonia. One of the key leaders of the political nationalist movement was Enric Prat de la Riba, who at the turn of the 20th century was the leader of *La Nacionalitat Catalana* from 1870 to 1917. He was an important figure in the political movement of reviving Catalan nationalism.

However, the ideological and political turmoil of the first third of the 20th century that eventually led to Civil War between the nationals (led by Franco) and the Republic (supporters of the Second Republic), ended in strict centralization and uniformity across the Spanish territories. As discussed above, this had profound effects on the Catalan educational system, in particular the ability to teach in Catalan and the freedom to teach courses for example on the history and culture of Catalonia. Still, Catalan education has a long history of innovation and pedagogical reform, which continued during the dictatorship under the leadership of famous *pedagogs*, such as Marta Mata i Garriga. These educationalists were significant in the development of a mass modern educational system in the post-Franco era.

The Political System and Its Environment

The reinvention of the Spanish state during the post-Franco era has been marked by the struggle for autonomy in Catalonia. According to Antoni Segura I Mas (2000), who wrote about the transition period in Spain, there are many similarities between the Second Republic and the years of the transition. He argued that between 1971 and 1975, there was increasing opposition to the Francoist values, the formation of social consensus in favor of political evolution in Spain, and the assassination of the Spanish Prime Minister and Franco supporter, Admiral Luis Carrero Blanco in 1973. In the years immediately following Franco's death in 1975, the transition included

the dismantling of institutions of the dictatorship (1976-1977); the legalization of political parties (1977); the proclamation of political amnesty, the violent and deadly attacks of the extreme Right; the celebration of general democratic elections and the victory of the Suárez party (1977); the restoration of the Generalitat and the Basque Council General (1977); the "sorgiment" of the new legality with the draft of the new Constitution (1978) that established the democratic State and the Statutes of Autonomy of Catalonia and the Basque Country (1979) and later, of Galicia and the rest of the communities; the celebration of the first democratic municipal elections and the second of the Spanish Parliament...[and] the first Parliamentary elections in Catalonia and the victories of the CiU and PNB, respectively (1980). (Segura I Mas, 2000, p. 20; my translation)

The Spanish Constitution of 1978 was developed as a guide for democratization.

With its intention that through the process of democratization, debates and new issues would create new avenues for change and revision, the Constitution remained rather ambiguous. In the construction of the Constitution, "where agreement could not be reached crucial issues were left ambiguous, to be resolved when democracy was fully consolidated" (Balfour, 2005, p. 4). This ambiguity continues to mark the relationship between Catalonia and the central state, including the 2006 revision of Catalonia's Statute of Autonomy.

The vague nature of the Constitution for the purpose of guiding decentralization has affected multiple areas of policy, including the development of education policy. Within the division of competencies between the regions, or CCAA, and the central state, there is a part that is exclusive to the Generalitat, which is considered to be outside of the area that is affected by fundamental right. The remainder is considered to be fundamental right, which is to be under the exclusive control of the state as protected by the Constitution. This has involved a number of conflicts brought to the Constitutional Tribunal over shared educational competencies between Catalonia and the Spanish state, and the exclusivity of Catalan competencies. These debates are linked to historical tensions over autonomy and independence, which are at the root of many debates between the four Catalan political parties (CiU, PSC, ICV, and ERC) since the transition to democracy.

Since 1980, the *Convergència i Unió* (CiU; Convergence and Union) party led by Jordi Pujol was the governing party in Catalonia until November of 2003. Throughout the 23 years, Pujol won each election without any interruption, and was seen as a very important political figure in the entire Spanish state, so important that he was often referred to as the "*de facto* vice-president of the [Spanish] government" after the PSOE relied heavily on Pujol and the CiU in the 1993 Spanish elections (Heywood, 1995, p. 245). Heywood (1995) described that during Pujol's "visit to Slovakia in the aftermath of its separation from the Czech Republic, he was treated as a head of state and the Catalan rather than the Spanish anthem was played" (p. 149). This might be considered to stand in contrast to the CiU's position in favor of Catalan autonomy, rather than the independence from Spain.

The CiU's position has been defined as moderate Catalan nationalist. Its existence began as a union of Jordi Pujol of the *Convergencia Democrática de Catalunya* (CDC) and Jordi Rigol i Roig of the *Unió Democrática de Catalunya* (UDC) in 1979. Self-defined as a Catalan nationalist party, the CiU's main goal was to extend Catalonia's level of self-government, yet in contrast to the *Esquerra Republicana de Catalunya*'s (ERC; Republic Left of Catalunya) position, it does not look towards full independence from the Spanish state. As Heywood (1995) argued, "for all Pujol's rhetoric about the Catalan nation, it has no pretensions to full independence" (p. 210). He went on to state, "pragmatic to the last, Pujol is mainly interested in ensuring that Catalonia derives the maximum benefit from Spain's system of regional government" (p. 210). CiU's position stands on unclear ground in its simultaneous support of a Catalan nation and unity of Spain. The use of terms, such as "self-determination" for Catalonia is often left unclear, in terms of what this might look like in the realities of policy-making. In opposition to the

CiU's position on Catalonia's relationship to Spain, other parties in Catalonia support independence for Catalonia. Of the four parties in Catalonia, the ERC, established in 1931, has maintained a more radical nationalist position on Catalan politics. Led by Josep Taradellas, the exiled leader of the Generalitat during the dictatorship, the ERC has a more secessionist position on Catalonia's relationship to Spain.

The CiU's leadership came to a close in the 2003 elections, with the retirement of Pujol and a combination of left-wing parties defeating the CiU for the first time. On November 16, 2003, Pasqual Maragall, head of the PSC became president of the Generalitat, while the ERC and the ICV-EUiA won parliamentary seats. This created a coalition between the *Partit dels Socialistes de Catalunya* (PSC; Socialists' Party of Catalunya), ERC, and *Iniciativa per Catalunya Verds* (ICV-EUiA; Initiative for Catalan Greens), known as the "Tripartite government," which was not always a smooth alliance. The broad agenda of the new Catalan government was a commitment to reforming Catalonia's Statute of Autonomy to increase the level of autonomy both within Spain and the EU. This included the struggle over greater educational competencies for Catalonia.

Following dispute over the final draft of Catalonia's Statute of Autonomy, the ERC left the Tripartite government, leading to an early election. In the 2006 election, the CiU won the largest number of parliamentary seats, but no party was able to win absolute majority. The leftist coalition has to date continued its presence, headed by José Montilla Aguilera of the PSC who became President of the Generalitat. A new party, *Ciutadans* (Citizens' Party), which has described itself as non-Catalan nationalist and center-left, also was developed and won some parliamentary seats. In these elections, debates over autonomy and independence have extended from the scene of Catalan elections into the rest of Spain.

In chapter 4, I trace these debates as they emerge in the politics of educational decentralization, and the 2006 revision of Catalonia's Statute of Autonomy. Across the long process of rapid and dramatic change that has occurred in 20th and 21st century Spain and Catalonia, education has been regarded and maintained as a central tool for both Catalan nationalism and Spanish unity. Yet, from recent literature on globalization and the development of a European education policy space, education also has increasingly been drawn into the discourses of the global economy, namely as it is thought to be related to the market and transnational capital. In this way, this project looks to understand the ways in which these recent developments are reflected in the production of education policy concerning decentralization in Catalonia, as pressures from the Spanish state, globalization, the EU, and the struggle for a Catalan nation intersect in complex ways.

CHAPTER 4

DECENTRALIZATION IN THE POST-FRANCO ERA

Earlier chapters have presented themes of globalization and nation state formation, fragmentary and integration pressures on nation states and shifts in educational governance. This chapter explores these issues further, through a discussion of the politics of state fragmentation, educational decentralization and the nature of the shifting relationship between Catalonia and the central Spanish state in the post-Franco era. Picking up the different modes and meanings of educational decentralization (political, administrative, and fiscal) from chapter 2, this chapter looks at nation state reformation and the implications for education policy from below.

Specifically, this chapter draws on the reflections of key policy-makers and government officials on the nature of the development of the Spanish decentralization model and its impact on education policy production both in Catalonia and Spain. Building on the previous chapter, this includes tracing the shifts in educational governance, particularly related to the unfolding of the Spanish state in the 1980s, 1990s and today. The perspective into the contemporary struggles for autonomy over education policy-making, from the perspective of regional actors in Catalonia and national policy actors in Spain, illustrates the complex intersections of language and culture extending across national and regional scales. These struggles represent a source of friction that must be placed in the context of both contemporary globalization debates and issues related to Europeanization of education.

ASYMMETRICAL DECENTRALIZATION

The tendency is always to decentralize. It is the craze, the way.
(Personal communication)

In the transition from the Francoist dictatorship to democracy, decentralization was a strategy employed by the Spanish state to meet the increasing pressures stemming from the historical nations (Catalonia and the Basque Country), and as means to consolidate the new democratic state. The Constitution of 1978 restructured the preexisting 50 provinces into a State of Autonomies, which established the 17 CCAA and two autonomous cities, Melilla and Ceuta. Closa and Heywood (2004) defined the democratic State of Autonomies as

a hybrid that attempts to meet three different (and to some extent contradictory) demands: first, the continued unity of the Spanish nation, inherited from its history as a strongly centralized state. Second, the recognition of the right to self-government of those regions with a strong sense of national identity....Third, the option for decentralization for other regions which aspired to autonomous self-government. (p. 84)

The division between regions with a strong national identity and regions with aspirations for self-government was defined early in the transition process as a way of guiding decentralization. In the process of decentralization, the autonomous communities (CCAA) were classified as either the

> nacionalidades (the Basques, th[e] Catalans and the Galicians), which can claim the status of 'historical nations', and regiones [the regions], which strive for autonomy on the basis of particular historical prerogatives (Navarre), their geography (the Balearics, the Canaries), or for socio-economic reasons (Andalusia, Extremadura, Valencia). (Börzel, 2002, p. 95)

With respect to the transfer of educational competencies to CCAA, it is worth noting that the decentralization process in Spain was not a blanket process, applied at the same time, in the same way in all 17 of the CCAA. Rather, the process of decentralization in Spain was asymmetrical, including in education.

In the transition period, the development of decentralization was uneven and therefore, the establishment of the new model of the Spanish state and powers allotted to the CCAA was not a smooth course of action. In fact, this process involved a contentious number of debates. Heywood (1995) argued, "it is... unsurprising that regionalism should have proved the single most contentious political issue during the post-Franco construction of democracy; nearly one-tenth of the lengthy Constitution is devoted to regional matters" (p. 142–143). It was decided that the three historical nations did not have to "make any formal application to the central state," as they were granted privileged status based on their respective Statutes of Autonomy established during the Second Republic (Heywood, 1995, p. 143). The other CCAA were divided into a grade one, the fast track, and grade two, the slow track.

Conflict and debate surrounded the process of decentralization, particularly as special circumstances were allowed for several of the CCAA. In the Spanish Constitution, Article 151 outlined an alternative route, in which any CCAA may "apply to receive the same high level of autonomy as the privileged regions, provided that a stringent series of conditions was first satisfied and the draft autonomy statute was subsequently endorsed in a referendum" (Heywood, 1995, p. 144). As described by Heywood (1995), after Catalonia's and the Basque Country's Statutes of Autonomy were approved by the central state in 1979, "there was an outbreak of so-called '*fiebre autonómica*' (autonomy fever) as all the remaining regions sought to establish regional governments," justified by Article 151 of the Constitution (p. 144; author's emphasis). Rather than follow the grade one and two process, Navarra, based on its particular history, was granted a "special route," while two CCAA (the Canary Islands, Valencia) were granted a status in between grades one and two (Heywood, 1995, p. 144). Furthermore, in the

Table 1. Process of educational decentralization

Category	CCAA
Historical nations (1979-1980)	Catalonia, Basque Country
Grade one/fast track (1981-1992)	Andalusia, Canary Islands, Valencia, Galicia, Navarra
Grade two/slow track (1992-2000)	Aragón, Asturias, Balearic Islands, Cantabria, Castilla-La Mancha, Castilla y León, Extremadura, La Rioja, Madrid, Murcia

asymmetrical process of decentralization, all CCAA chose the option of full political autonomy over administrative autonomy, which created both competition and tension among the CCAA. Table 1 provides an illustration of the three stages of educational governance and the legal transfer of educational competencies from the central state to the CCAA.

Unity and Diversity?

On the millennium, the final decision-making authorities were transferred to the remaining CCAA, constituting Spain as one of the most politically decentralized states in Europe (Hanson, 2000). Pereyra (2002) wrote "in theory, these reorganisations seek to maintain a balance between unity and diversity through coordination, cooperation and collaboration" (p. 668). As such, there were hopes of intergovernmental cooperation between the different CCAA. With all CCAA opting for full political autonomy, the state moved to equalize levels of autonomy across all CCAA. This invoked widespread conflicts among the CCAA over claims that particular CCAA were receiving greater privileges through the decentralization process, including on issues such as taxation. Börzel (2002) argued that the Spanish central state's attempts to equalize all levels of autonomy across the state

> further reduced the privileged status that the three *nacionalidades* had initially enjoyed. The policy of 'café para todos' (coffee for everyone) as opposed to 'champagne for the *nacionalidades*'…profoundly challenged the preferential status and caused substantial conflicts between the *nacionalidades* and the central state. (p. 95)

This also caused both competition and resentment between the CCAA.

Those on the slower track of decentralization appeared to resent the privileges seemingly provided to the historical nations (Börzel, 2002). Even among the historical nations, there was a lack of intergovernmental cooperation. Börzel (2002) reported that Catalonia regularly complained that the "Basques and the Navarese are 'given brandy with their coffee'" in the form of taxation privileges" (p. 95).

These tensions escalated during the decentralization process of Spanish public institutions, as they required fiscal restructuring to support and equalize the transition of authorities to the CCAA.

The financial inequality across the 17 CCAA also became a central issue of debate in the decentralization process. In the new funding system, the CCAA were each allotted grants from the central government to provide funding for public administrative costs of education, health, and transportation. The block grant funding system, along with the Inter-Territorial Compensation Funds (FCI), which sought to decrease the economic inequity between wealthy and more impoverished regions, helped to increase the public expenditure on education to over 5% of Spain's Gross Domestic Product (GDP) by 1996 (Edge, 2000). This is a dramatic increase from the 2.6% expenditure on education in 1981 (Hanson, 2000; Torres & Piña, 2004). The FCI "was initially distributed according to a formula based upon relative levels of income, migration, and unemployment rates" (Heywood, 1995, p. 152–153). However, issues of migration from other parts of Spain to Catalonia caused a reevaluation of the FCI structure. Wealthier CCAA, such as Catalonia, have also resented the FCI given their higher contributions, and what they have been provided in return.

In attempts to gain greater regional competencies, the CCAA overall have not been able come together to form a cooperative relationship that would allow them greater collective bargaining power with the central Spanish state. When asked about the level of cooperation that exists between the CCAA, one government official responded "Inexistent. Inexistent....The state intervenes a lot because whatever collaborative agreement made between the CCAA, there has to be approval from the Parliament" (personal communication). In order for the CCAA to begin to form more cooperative relationships with one another, they need the support of the central state. In this way, the central state maintains an authoritative position, which limits the intergovernmental cooperation between the CCAA. Consequently, the conflict, competition, and the independent "*cada una por su cuenta*" (to each their own) policies of the CCAA has limited their mobilization for greater autonomy from the central state (Börzel, 2002, p. 102).

Shaping the Decentralization Process

Political decentralization was a central mode of governance advocated in Spain to meet the regional demands of Catalonia and the Basque Country for greater autonomy, decision-making, and the revival of historical rights. Political decentralization also was perceived as a vehicle for greater democratization and local empowerment. At a crucial stage in the shift from a strict authoritarian dictatorship to a democratic organization, a political form of decentralization was deemed necessary for the consolidation of the democratic Spanish state. An education policy-maker stated, "giving more competencies to the autonomies has been important in order to get the administration closer to the citizenry. The closer to the citizen, the better" (personal communication). In this way, a political form of decentralization was assumed to be a core ingredient to the successful continuation of the process of democratization. With the adoption of the Spanish Constitution into law, it was widely considered by politicians, citizens, and scholars to be the backbone of Spain's efforts of democratization.

The Spanish Constitution (1978) outlines the division of competencies between the CCAA and the central state. In the current decentralized Spanish state structure, the division of power between the central government and the CCAA can be divided into three levels, those exclusive the state, those exclusive to the CCAA, and those that are shared between the state and the CCAA. In the drafting of the Spanish Constitution, Articles 148 and 149 illustrate the jurisdiction and the division of competencies between the CCAA and the state. Article 148 states that CCAA may take on responsibility over self-government, territorial planning and housing, environmental protection, and the promotion of economic development within the national economic framework, museums and libraries of interest to the CCAA, monuments, and the promotion of culture, research, and teaching of the regional language. Article 149 section 1 and section 1a state that the state has exclusive jurisdiction over the regulation of basic conditions that guarantee equality of all Spanish citizens to exercise their constitutional rights.

Article 149 sections 2a-3a states that the central state also has exclusive competency over nationality, immigration, international relations, national defense and the Armed Forces, general planning of economic policy, the protection of Spain's cultural and artistic heritage, museums, libraries and archives of the state, regulation of conditions relative to obtaining, issuing and standardization of academic degrees, and statistics for state purposes. The final section of Article 149 states that competencies not expressively attributed to the state by the Constitution will correspond to the CCAA, in line with their respective Statutes of Autonomy. Competencies that are not assumed by the Statutes of Autonomy will correspond to the state.

One of the most complex issues of governance fall into the area of shared competencies between the state and CCAA. Education is interpreted to lie within this area, in which the Ministry of Education, Social Policy and Sport (MEPSYD), formally known as the Ministry of Education and Science (MEC) shares educational responsibilities with the CCAA. According to the MEC (n.d.),

> the Spanish Constitution of 1978 and the Statutes of Autonomy ensure that the common elements of education policy and the Spanish educational system will be directed by the MEC, and cooperatively managed by the MEC and the respective Ministries of Education in each of the CCAA that already have had educational competencies transferred to them. (para. 1; my translation)

Due to the complexity of shared educational competencies, and the ambiguity of the Constitution, there has been an overall challenge of whether Spain "would have one educational system made up of 17 integrated, semi-autonomous parts rather than 17 separate educational systems" (Hanson, 2000, p. 20). In response to this challenge and regional pressures for greater educational autonomy, the central Spanish state established a system, in which educational responsibilities over policy production would be divided across three levels: central state, CCAA, and local administration.

The Spanish state's structures of administration include the MEPSYD, the *Alta Inspección* (High Inspectorate) in each CCAA, and the provincial offices in Melilla and Ceuta. The powers allotted to the central administration include the regulation of the entire state system in order to standardize and unify the Spanish education system, international and European cooperation in the area of education, evaluation and inspection through the authority of the *Alta Inspección*, the regulation of teacher and other professional qualifications, and the establishment of minimum educational requirements for each center of education. The MEPSYD specifically controls basic educational legislation, accreditation of certificates and degrees, general planning of the education system, and the determination and maintenance of minimum requirements for common curriculum areas, especially those of national concern, such as Spanish history, Spanish national language, mathematics, and science.

The implementation of educational policies dictated by the central state and the remainder of educational responsibilities, such as the design of academic programs to support cultural, linguistic, and economic development of regional communities, is reserved for the CCAA. Additionally, a system of shared curricular control between the central state and CCAA has been established in the post-Franco era. This system of shared control is regulated through a system of "minimum academic requirements" or "minimums." The system of minimums mandates that 65% of the curriculum of secondary schools (55% in CCAA with another language, such as in Catalonia) must reflect a national (Castilian) focus, and the remaining 35% is left up to the individual CCAA. It is noteworthy that not all of the CCAA have adopted a decentralized educational program. Pereyra (2002) noted, "some autonomous regions have adopted central programmes, so that instead of having a single centralist state, there are now several centralist autonomous governments" (p. 668). This provides for extensive complexity in the asymmetrical form of educational decentralization currently undertaken in Spain.

Drawing back on the discussion in the previous chapter, the development of the Spanish educational system is characterized by state legislation in the form of a new or reconstituted organic law, which the CCAA are then charged with implementing. In the Constitution, Article 27 section 1 states that "everyone has the right to education," and Article 27 section 2 states, "the objective of education shall aim at the full development of the human personality in respect for the democratic principles of coexistence and the basic rights and liberties" (Spanish Constitution, 1978, Section 27, para. 1–2). As described by an educational authority in Barcelona, "the Constitution states that the central government guarantees basic, fundamental rights to its citizens through organic laws, which affect the entire state" (personal communication). While the curriculum is divided out into a system of minimums, with Catalonia able to utilize 55% of the total curriculum, Catalonia cannot generate its own law of education independent from Spain. In other words, as one education policy-maker in Barcelona stated, "the organic laws always affect the whole of Spain. The organic law has to be applied, so when the law is approved, the Autonomous Communities have to apply it" (personal communication). Without actual legislative control to produce policy independent from the central Spanish state, Catalonia's power stems from essentially how it implements the central law. One educational expert in Catalonia indicated,

> the Autonomous Communities have very little margin to innovate in education. Catalonia does not have its own law of education, which from a nationalist perspective, means that the state has not left any space in which CCAA and the state might have equal footing. (personal communication)

The other issue with the CCAA's implementation of the organic laws is the rapid changes made in educational legislation with each new political stage of the post-Franco era. With six laws passed in little more than three decades, the CCAA have been consumed by constant educational changes to implement: "what has happened is that ultimately the educational laws change so often that right when we are implementing the organic law, there is already a revision to the law" (personal communication). Even among the rapid changes, government officials and policy-makers in Barcelona argued that Catalonia has not gained any additional autonomy legislatively to produce policy.

LOAPA

In the many changes that have taken place during the transition period, there were a number of tensions between the CCAA themselves and between the central state and CCAA over the division of competencies. As a consequence of these issues and *Euskadi Ta Askatasuna*'s (ETA; Basque separatist group) numerous attacks on the central government at different times during the decentralization process, there appeared to be a level of insecurity felt by central state. In 1981, the central government, under the leadership of the UCD, presented the LOAPA (Organic Law for the Harmonization of the Process of Self-Government, also known as the Law of Harmonization). The LOAPA represented an attempt to slow down the process of decentralization and make it more gradual.

The LOAPA essentially "limited the areas under the exclusive jurisdiction of the self-governing communities and marked the beginning of the retrieval of powers by the central government," even in the historical nations of Catalonia and the Basque Country (Balcells, 1996, p. 179). Heywood (1995) wrote that the proposition of the LOAPA established that in issues of conflict, "state law was always to prevail over regional [CCAA] law" (p. 145). The LOAPA generated heavy opposition, particularly from Catalonia and the Basque Country. These regions immediately brought the issue to the Constitutional Tribunal. The argument of Catalonia and the Basque Country was that the LOAPA would remove their privileged CCAA status and put them both on the equivalent level with the CCAA at grade two of the decentralization process (Heywood, 1995). Ultimately, the Constitutional Tribunal declared in 1983 that over one-third of the LOAPA was unconstitutional.

One of the major consequences of the LOAPA relates to its impact on the relationship between the central state and Catalonia. First, after the ruling of the Constitutional Tribunal, it became evident that Catalonia and the Basque Country were powerful and could not be ignored by the central state over issues pertaining to their autonomous rights, particularly in the process of creating a democratic State of Autonomies. Heywood (1995) claimed that the "judgment on the LOAPA ensured that the new government [PSOE] would have to accommodate the demands of the politically significant regions, most notably the Basque Country and Catalonia" (p. 145). Nonetheless, as argued by Balcells (1996), and contended by a number of government officials and policy makers in interviews, the central state found a legal route around the LOAPA that still achieved the central state's goals of greater centralized authority. Balcells (1996) wrote, "the State did not need to resort to the Law of Harmonization since it could attain the same objective by means of the *leyes de bases* (organic laws) over which it holds the sole prerogative" (p. 192). Balcells (1996) went on to argue that the state

> has succeeded...in gradually undermining the jurisdiction of the self-governing communities through the widespread use of the leyes de bases whose function is not to establish general guidelines for the self-governing communities, but to define matters reserved to the State on account of their importance, the precise degree of importance being determined by the central government itself. (p. 192)

This issue is discussed further from the perspective of system actors interviewed in Barcelona. Apart from the LOAPA and the development of exclusive competencies over organic laws, another state governance strategy that many system actors discussed in interviews was the *Alta Inspección*.

Alta Inspección

In order for the Spanish state to negotiate simultaneous pressures of consolidating democratization and asymmetrical decentralization in the process of education policy production, it has utilized the *Alta Inspección* (High Inspectorate). The *Alta Inspección* is an inspection of all school systems by the central government to ensure that they are accountable for central state standards in education. It is a way of maintaining accountability and standarization across all CCAA. According to the MEPSYD, the *Alta Inspección* was developed in the context of the new political organization of the Spanish State of Autonomies. It is based on Article 27.8 of the Spanish Constitution, which arranges the inspection and standardization of education between the different administrative powers.

Through evaluation, the MEPSYD can direct and manage the implementation of policies in the Spanish educational system. In a description of the *Alta Inspección*, the then MEC (n.d.) stated that it "is based on cooperation with the CCAA, and is, above all, a very important factor in the social solidarity and political vertebra of the State" (http://www.mec.es/educa/jsp/plantilla.jsp?area=ccaa&id=31, para. 2; my translation). The *Alta Inspección* also can be interpreted as a mechanism of control. An educational leader in Catalonia explained, "the *Alta Inspección* is like the central state's medium of control over the Autonomous Communities in order to evaluate and ensure that the competencies that they give to the Autonomous

Communities are being implemented properly" (personal communication). In this way, although implementation is meant to be left to the CCAA, the central state exercises its central authority through the *Alta Inspección*.

The *Alta Inspección* was first created in the 1979 Statutes of Autonomy of Catalonia and the Basque Country during the process of decentralization. Rubio (2000) explained,

> the *Alta Inspección*, as a function connected to the educational competencies reserved for the [Spanish] state, was introduced in the Statutes of Autonomy of each CCAA that received absolute or total educational competencies (initially Catalonia and the Basque Country). (p. 71; my translation)

The *Alta Inspección* was originally intended to protect and guarantee the educational functions and competencies of the central state. When asked about the current role of the *Alta Inspección* within education in Catalonia, some policy-makers and educational leaders argued that it had no impact. For example, one educational leader in Catalonia described the *Alta Inspección* as a group of inspectors that "are interested as observers in order to monitor what is happening... as external observers in this case" (personal communication). Another government official took the opposite viewpoint and argued that the *Alta Inspección* is one of the most important instruments that the central administration possesses: "it is the instrument that the administration has in order to be able to modify or transform the reality" of education in Catalonia (personal communication).

Another education policy-maker referred to the *Alta Inspección* as merely a "symbolic figure" of authority in the compliance and implementation of Spanish educational legislation (personal communication). This participant went on to argue that it potentially could be used to control and steer education in Catalonia. However, because of a political agreement between the CiU of Catalonia and the central government, the *Alta Inspección* essentially had no real significance. This participant stated that there is an "implicit pact between the CiU and the central government that there would be the *Alta Inspección* but that it would not be used" (personal communication). The example of the *Alta Inspección* sheds light on the mechanisms that the modern state uses to exercise authority.

As the Spanish state has undergone dramatic reterritorialization under strategies of political, administrative, and fiscal decentralization, the state has used strategies to exercise its power and authority. These include the development of the LOAPA early in the process of decentralization and the development of exclusive rights to establish organic laws of education. I argue that the *Alta Inspección* is one such strategy. Even if symbolic, the state maintains an authoritative role in the supervision of Catalonia and other CCAA on their compliance with central policy objectives and educational legislation. Following the work of Balcells (1996), the LOAPA can be interpreted as an unsuccessful legislative strategy of the central state to slow down the process of decentralization. In the failure of the LOAPA, the state has adopted additional measures, such as the *Alta Inspección*, through which to exercise authority over areas of educational governance.

EDUCATIONAL DECENTRALIZATION IN CATALONIA

At the level of the CCAA are the Ministries and Departments of Education that represent the CCAA. These government structures are charged with overseeing the portion of the curriculum allocated to the regional level of the CCAA, the creation of centers, and staff administration. In each of the CCAA, there is a local administration that is usually represented by municipal structures, which control aspects of education such as ensuring compliance with obligatory education and the maintenance of infant and primary education.

Given that the CCAA interpret and administer policies dictated by the central state, the form of educational decentralization appears to represent a functional model of decentralization. As an authority on legislative issues in Spain and Catalonia explained during an interview:

> The Constitutional Tribunal interpreted education as a shared competency, in which the state dictates mandates through the organic law, which includes all of the basic norms, such as the right to education. Then, the CCAA are charged with implementation of these mandates. That is to say that education policy development functions constitutionally as something shared without actually being shared, but it is the interpretation that they have given it. (personal communication)

In this case, the central state creates national legislation dictated by Article 148, Section 1, and the CCAA are then charged with implementing these norms. Here, the participant is arguing that while the Constitutional Tribunal has interpreted education as shared, legislative control remains under the authority of the central state.

The MEPSYD claims to control only aspects over basic educational legislation in order to guarantee the basic rights to education. However, there are many cases in which regional CCAA policy-makers and system actors have interpreted state education policy production as an extension of central state control into the terrain of CCAA competencies. For example, a high level authority in Catalonia explained that

> It can no longer be claimed that these [central state policies] are just the basic norms because they have completely invaded the terrain of the Autonomous competencies. In other words, if it [the central state] ends up regulating things like the size of letters in textbooks, the number of pages that the textbooks should have…it is clear that they are regulating aspects that are not basic principles, that are not rights, but rather they are regulating aspects of education that are competencies of the CCAA. (personal communication)

Even the ways in which policies are implemented in CCAA are regulated by the state. An educational leader in Catalonia concisely stated, "the state does the determining," (personal communication). During an interview with an educational leader in Catalonia, the participant referred to the example of the higher educational system in Catalonia and Spain to illustrate the way in which education policy is produced. This participant stated that the CCAA have full competencies in the management of their universities, but the state decides what they can do...the central Ministry really is in a perfect situation, because makes all policies but it has no responsibilities at all over the implementation of the decisions it makes...[the Ministry says] 'tomorrow, every professor has to earn double. Great ok' and they write it and send it to the Communities. (personal communication)

These views sharply contrasted those from educational officials and policymakers in the central state government in Madrid, who argued that the areas of policy in which Catalonia and the other CCAA were responsible made the Spanish system as one of the most decentralized national systems of education in Europe and the world (personal communication).

Participants in Madrid and a few educational authorities in Catalonia cited the Sectoral Conferences (*Conferencias Sectoriales*) as a mechanism that the state has adopted for encouraging greater participation from Catalonia in policy-making decisions. The Sectoral Conferences emerged out of the LOAPA as a way in which officials of the central state could cooperate and coordinate with CCAA leaders "in order to maximize intergovernmental cooperation and to avoid conflicts" (Moreno, 2002, p. 405). One participant argued that during the process of decentralization

one of the problems that [policymakers and government officials] detected in the 1980s was that there were no institutions of dialogue between the CCAA and the central state, so with LOAPA, the Sectoral Conferences were established to exist as a type of intergovernmental conferences. (personal communication)

Each Sectoral Conference consists of the Minister of Education and representatives from each of the 17 CCAA.

The Director General of Territorial Cooperation and High Inspectorate of the MEPSYD act as a secretary at the meetings although they cannot participate in voting matters. The Sectoral Conference functions as a way in which to encourage the exchange of information, increase intergovernmental participation, propose educational policies that guarantee the basic equality of citizens, determine collaborative projects, examine performance indicators, and exchange and compile data from each of the CCAA in order to construct a profile of how the state of Spain is proceeding in meeting EU educational criteria.

While Catalonia is represented in the Sectoral Conferences, one participant argued that the scope and agenda of the Sectoral Conference itself is under authority of the central government. The participant stated, "the Sectoral Conferences are controlled by the central government because it is the central government that has the capacity to establish the agenda" (personal communication). In the Spanish state's attempts to establish intergovernmental relationships with the CCAA, it seems to rely primarily on vertical relations, with power extending from the central state to the CCAA. These vertical relations have been interpreted by system actors at the level of Catalonia to be unidirectional emanating from the state to the CCAA. An educational expert in Catalonia reflected on this issue,

> I think that the CCAA have much less trust for the state than the state does of the CCAA for one basic reason. The state, through legislation, can have much more of an effect on the CCAA....The state has many means to intervene in the CCAA... If they [the state] have everything already done and made, such as the law of education, what are we going to say? You can see the lack of trust much more from the CCAA towards the central government basically for this reason. (personal communication)

Given Spain's history, the relationship between Catalonia and the central state from the perspective of system actors in Catalonia seems to reflect a level of suspicion and distrust towards the central state. In discussions of decentralization, this issue also appeared to be reflected in a system actors' uneasiness over fiscal matters.

As discussed in chapter 2, fiscal decentralization is often advocated in conditions in which the central state is unable economically to supply adequate public expenditure in education. Although pressures vary, many state systems around the world show an increase in fiscal decentralization. Paqueo and Lammert (2000) argued that decentralization is often employed as it is thought to

> generate revenues for the education system by taking advantage of local sources of taxation, as well as reduce operating costs. In this model, the goal is to shift some of the financial burden for education to the regional or local government, community organizations, and/or parents....It also assumes that more active involvement by more social institutions and groups will lead to an increase in resources available for education. (p. 1)

In the decentralized post-Francoist Spanish state, the CCAA pay capital tax and collect income tax, while the central state exercises authority over education policy production. As one educational expert in Catalonia explained, "the State legislates, the Autonomous Communities pay" (personal communication). Even with increased fiscal responsibilities at CCAA levels, the central Spanish state maintains an important role in policy production, which has particular implications for CCAA decision-making.

In a discussion of fiscal decentralization, one educational leader in Barcelona described the necessity for the state to yield particular decision-making powers to Catalonia because of its responsibility financially. The educational leader in Barcelona argued,

> because we have to pay, we need to have something to say. The important things, we cannot decide, and if there are leftovers, we can eat the leftovers. We pay for the cake, and sometimes we get to decide what to do with the leftovers. (personal communication)

The CCAA are increasingly responsible for fiscal matters, although it appears that they remain steered by the state in matters of policy decision-making and standard-setting. This leaves the CCAA to gain little autonomy over education policy-making matters. As often is the case in functional forms of decentralization, decision-making at local and regional levels is not enhanced by the increase in responsibilities over the collection and distribution of finances.

Conflict and Contestation

In Spain's efforts of democratization, the decentralization of Spanish institutions, including education, has not been an on-going smooth process without interruption or contestation. Conflicts continue to surface between the historical nations, particularly Catalonia and the Basque Country, and the central state. One example deals directly with educational decentralization in Catalonia and the establishment of minimums, in which the Catalan government took steps to deny the central government's laws in areas of curricula, regarding them as a threat to Catalonia's autonomy (Ferrer, 2000; Hanson, 2000).

In October of 1997, the MEC, as it was known then, under the leadership of the PP, passed a decree placing the humanities curriculum (Spanish language, history, geography, and literature) under center state control (Hanson, 2000). However, the President of the Catalan government and head of the CiU party, Jordi Pujol, declared that the region would "practice civil disobedience and absolutely refuse to implement the new humanities policy" (Hanson, 2000, p. 38). Pujol also threatened to remove his alliance with the PP if the humanities education policy was not significantly altered (Hanson, 2000). The above example of Catalonia is just one among many illustrations of the tension that exists in Spain's negotiation of local and regional differences and national imperatives.

In the development of the decentralized system of governance, the Constitutional Tribunal has served as judicial grounds for conflict between the central Spanish state and the CCAA. A high number of conflict cases have been brought to the Constitutional Tribunal. Börzel (2002) wrote that as of the year 2002, "Constitutional conflict is still more prevalent in Spanish intergovernmental relations than in other decentralized countries" (p. 101). This is a primary example of the confrontation, competition, and conflict that dominates the decentralized structure of the Spanish state. Although often considered and praised as a "miracle model," these examples show the intersection and clash of various policy pressures in education, demonstrating that local, regional, central state priories do not always align neatly with one another.

Additionally, in the decentralized system of education, key policy debates appear to stem from the lack of intergovernmental cooperation and the competition that exists between the CCAA. The tensions that arise between the CCAA and the central state, as well as among the CCAA themselves, have continued to mount, particularly around the new 2006 Catalan Statute of Autonomy and the signing of the 2006 National Pact for Education in Catalonia. Both of these were developed in highly politicized environments. In interviews in Barcelona and Madrid, these were central topics of reflection. I begin with the process of drafting, revising, and approving the new *Estatut de Autonomia* (Statute of Autonomy) in Catalonia.

EL ESTATUT

In the process of democratization and part of constitutional law, Catalonia established a Statute of Autonomy in 1979, in order to represent the individual rights, capacities, and responsibilities of the citizens of Catalonia. The Statute of

Autonomy also worked to delineate the relationship between the central state and the CCAA over legislative issues of policy production. This relationship is defined by the competencies that both the central state and the CCAA possess, and the political institutions and financing at the level of the CCAA. After Catalonia's 1714 loss of independence to the central Spanish state, as described in chapter 3, many attempts were made to regenerate the autonomous institutions of the Catalan government. One of these efforts was the 1932 Statute of Autonomy of Catalonia, which was brought to life during the democratically elected Second Republic from 1931 to 1936.

In the Second Republic, national communities, such as Catalonia and the Basque Country were formally recognized. In 1931, on the same day as the Second Republic was declared, Francesc Macià, a leader of the nationalist movement in Catalonia, also made a public declaration for a Catalan Republic and an Iberian Confederation. This led to a Statute of Autonomy for Catalonia, and the recovery of the Generalitat, the Catalan government. During the Francoist dictatorship, the regional government and all of the developments in regional institutions were disbanded and outlawed. Following Franco's death in 1975, Catalonia pushed to have the Generalitat reestablished once again, which was promulgated in 1977. The 1979 Statute of Autonomy of Catalonia, the Statute of Sau, was aligned with the process of democratization, the Constitution of 1978, and the construction of the State of Autonomies in Spain.

There was an unwritten pledge during the development of the 1978 Constitution that included the potential for future revisions to the structure of the State of Autonomies. This also included the possibility that each CCAA could revise their respective Statutes of Autonomy. During the 23 years of the CiU government's reign in Catalonia during the post-Franco era, there was a conservative, nationalist perspective aimed to extend Catalonia's level of self-government, but not seek independence from the Spanish state.

The move to revise the 1979 Statute of Autonomy was not a political project until the new Tripartite government took office in 2003. Also in 2003, a study was produced by a group of researchers at the Institute of Autonomous Studies, which marked the 25th Anniversary of the 1979 Statute. In the 2003 report, *Informe Sobre la Reforma del Estatuto*, the authors analyzed the objectives and goals set out by the Statute with respect to the previous 25 years, and concluded that many of these goals still were not reached. A member of the Catalan government stated, "the conclusion was not very positive in the sense that there were so many expectations, so much hope and so many ideas in 1979 that we thought we [Catalan citizens] would be able to achieve" (personal communication). The report laid out several important deficits. One of these deficits was the extent to which the exclusive competencies of the Generalitat of Catalonia were actually exclusive, which in the report, the authors concluded were actually fragmented between the central state and Catalonia.

The other deficits fell under the umbrella of Catalan nationalism and identity. This related to the perceived inequality between Catalan culture and language, and Spanish culture and Castilian Spanish. One authority in the government in Catalonia stated: "perhaps in 1979, we could imagine that the two would be equal, but now we have seen that this is not the case" (personal communication). Another pressure driving the new Statute of Autonomy is the existence of the EU. Government officials, policy-makers and other system actors pointed to the idea of the new Statute as a way to be able to look towards and learn from other EU regions, particularly those with powerful representation in their central state governments.

Based on these deficits, a draft of a revised Statute was developed. An authority on legal issues in Catalonia described the legal process as "all about precision, detailing and removing" what is exclusive to the Generalitat from the central state (personal communication). This participant went on to state that

the objective is to separate [what is a competency of the Generalitat in Catalonia] and what was not happening, happens now that the state is [decentralized] and the original drafting of the 1979 Statute is very ambiguous, [for example] 'full competency of educational matters,' well of course what happened has happened, so to avoid all of this, we have to go to the other extreme of detail, precision, and continuing to separate. (personal communication)

In 2003, one of the primary projects of the new Tripartite government in Catalonia was to extend Catalonia's autonomy. Furthermore, in 2004, under the new Socialist leadership of President Zapatero, the possibility opened for Catalonia to begin negotiations with the central state for a new Statute of Autonomy.

As a result, Catalonia's Statute of Autonomy was substituted by the new project for the Statute of Autonomy of Catalonia. The central discourse emanating from the Catalan government was, "Because these are new times. New challenges. New Statute" and "The times are changing. Change the Statute." (Generalitat de Catalunya, 2005c, para. 1; my translation). The government's central slogan of new times and new challenges signifies just how much has transpired in three decades since the transition to democracy. Catalonia now must confront economic, political and cultural globalization, and deal with the significance of a Catalan national identity and the challenges of increased global mobility. Yet, the slogan also points to the need for greater change in the democratic Spanish state, including the need for greater rights of self-government.

The revision of the Statute of Autonomy was one of the most important topics of Spanish politics since its approval in 2005, and one of the most political in Spain. Of the contested issues involved in this project was the discourse surrounding the official recognition of Catalonia as a nation and Spain as a plurinational state. Other political issues included the deepening of autonomy over governance responsibilities of the Catalan government and the potential to further accentuate the rescaling of the Spanish state. From the perspective of many Catalan citizens, there was a hope that the new Statute would allow Catalonia to

enter negotiations on a new framework that would see a single administration in Catalonia which, in addition to the control it already has over education, culture, health and policing, would have the final say on public finances and be represented separately from Spain in the EU and at other international bodies. (Bale, 2005, p. 42)

In an interview with an educational leader of a local educational agency in Barcelona stated,

> even if we continue to increase the level of competencies [of the Catalan government], you have to logically realize that we are in a Spanish state that is formed for a series of autonomies but with everything that we have, like Catalonia, Basque Country, Galicia, or Navarra, with distinct cultures but in no case are they contrary... I am not going to hide if I tell you that what I would like is a federal state, I would not like to have an independent country. I am very happy inside a Spanish state but with a Catalonia that has many more competencies, with a lot more power to be able to do and give more services to its citizens. (personal communication)

In the drafting of the new Statute of Autonomy in Catalonia, questions of Catalan nationalism, autonomy, and even independence once again were brought to the forefront of political debate.

The discourse surrounding the use of the concept, nation, was particularly debated in Spain, which has been a well-ingrained debate in Spain. In the post-Franco era, over the past two decades Catalonia's case for nationhood has involved international attention. For example, the 1992 summer Olympic Games took place in Barcelona, with the President of Catalonia's CiU party, Jordi Pujol "claim[ing] the triumph of the Barcelona Olympic Games for the 'nation' of Catalonia" (Heywood, 1995, p. 149). When the new Statute was drafted in 2005, with an overwhelming vote from the Catalan Parliament in favor of the new Statute, the "nation of Catalonia" was included in Article 1.

Article 1 stated: "Catalonia is a nation that exercises its self-government constituted as an autonomous community in accordance with the Constitution and with this Estatut, which is its basic institutional law" (Generalitat de Catalunya, 2006c, Preliminary Title, Article 1, para. 1). The revised draft of the Statute of Autonomy originally used the language of a plurinational Spanish state and a Catalonia nation. It also established that Catalonia, based on historical rights, has developed a unique position with respect to its language, culture, civil law and territorial organization. During the negotiations that took place at the national Spanish level, where the Statute subsequently had to be approved, notions of a Catalan nation and a plurinational Spain came under intense fire outside of Catalonia.

Many of Catalonia's efforts to gain greater autonomy over political domains, including education, have resulted in a backlash of attitudes against the Catalan language and culture, what one participant, a high ranked authority in the central government in Madrid, called "*catalanofobia*" (catalanophobia). More broadly, the anti-Catalanism movement in Spain encompasses particular political opposition to Catalan nationalism, which is seen as synonymous with the independence of Catalonia from Spain. One example is the launching of España 2000, a right wing political organization aimed at maintaining the unity of Spain above all else. The leaders and members of the organization maintain a pro-nationalist position standing against the granting of greater autonomy to CCAA, like Catalonia. The

España 2000 (n.d.) stated, "National solidarity is the necessary cement between members of the same community" (para. 1). These tensions have brought the spotlight on education, which have led to a number of debates over educational competencies, including the particular focus of the curriculum, language choice, and control over governance.

However, as argued by the Generalitat, the use of rhetoric of a Catalan nation was purposefully not connected with the discourse of the state or issues of sovereignty, and did not contradict the principles of Article 2 of the Spanish Constitution, which states

> the Constitution declares itself 'based upon the indissoluble unity of the Spanish Nation, the common and indivisible *patria* of all Spaniards, and recognizes and guarantees the right to autonomy of the nationalities and regions forming it and solidarity between all of them.' (Guibernau, 2006, p. 217)

Even in an attempt to align with the logic proposed by Brassloff (1996) who wrote, "a Catalan's state is Spain, his nation is Catalonia," these terms were nonetheless highly controversial (p. 113). The Catalan proposal came under heavy criticism from Madrid and the rest of the Spanish state, especially the Spanish right. For example, the PP rejected the project from the very beginning claiming that it was against the legal basis of the Spanish Constitution of 1978 and that it threatened the political unity of Spain. The leader of the PP, Mariano Rajoy criticized the revised Statute of Autonomy as "an outrageous fraud" (Mead, 2006, p. 18). The uneasiness surrounding the Statute revolved around the potential for Catalonia to gain grounds for independence. Consequently, throughout Spain, there were four levels of boycotts staged that were targeted at Catalan products, such as cava, and Catalan banks that supported Catalonia's revised Statute of Autonomy.

Most controversial was the reaction to the revised Statute by Lieutenant General José Mena Aguado of the Spanish military. Lieutenant Aguado claimed that if Catalonia established itself as a nation, the Spanish army had every right to treat Catalonia as independent from Spain and invade Catalan territory. Given the long history of Spain's violent and oppressive military invasions in Catalonia, Lieutenant Aguado's comments brought these historical tensions to the forefront of debates over the Statute of Autonomy. As Mead (2006) pointed out, "it is only 25 years ago since the last attempted *coup d'etat* in Spain was led by Army officers who were against the process of democratization taking place in the wake of Franco's death" (p. 18). The revised Statute of Autonomy became deeply embedded in a long-standing, contentious history of Spain. The debates over the Statute of Autonomy in Catalonia also returned to the familiar autonomy versus independence discussion.

Given the complexity surrounding the term, nation, as well as the political contestation between Catalonia and the central government, the official declaration of Catalonia as a nation within the new Statute of Autonomy raised historical insecurities regarding the political, economic, social, and cultural unity of the Spanish state. Ultimately, the word nation was later removed during negotiations in Madrid, before the final Catalan citizen vote. Article 1 of the Statute now reads,

"Catalonia, as a nationality, exercises its constituted self-government as an autonomous community in accordance with the Constitution and this Statute" (Generalitat de Catalunya, 2006c, Preliminary Title, Article 1, para. 1). Nation, which appeared to be equated with independence in the political debates and media coverage of the revision of Catalonia's Statute of Autonomy, was subsequently changed to nationality. A legal advisor in the drafting of the revised Statute of Autonomy in Catalonia stated

> my personal opinion is that legally [the word nation] did not have any importance, it is not totally unconstitutional because nation is used both in Spanish and Catalan. It has many definitions, many of which are historically rooted in different points of view, so [nation] can mean many things depending on the context....the affirmation that Catalonia is a nation did not have any legal consequences, but it is clear that politically, for today's government, the PSOE, it was unacceptable. (personal communication)

In this case, rather than possess any legal consequences, the symbolism of nation became the center of debate. Ultimately, the concept nation was reserved in its meaning found in Article 2 of the Spanish Constitution, and it was replaced by nationality in Catalonia's Statute of Autonomy.

Political Discourse

As the political discourse mounted leading up to the vote on the Statute, language and language policy became one of the more politicized issues. Legal advisors to the draft of the revised Statute, Catalan nationalists, and other organizations supported the inclusion of several articles in the Statute that sought to equalize Catalan with Castilian Spanish. Article 6.1 of the 2006 Statute of Autonomy (Generalitat de Catalunya, 2006c) states

> the language of Catalonia is Catalan. As such, Catalan is the language of normal and preferred use in public administrations and means of public communication in Catalonia, and it is also the language normally used as the lingua franca and the language of instruction.

In the Statute, Article 6.2 states, "Catalan is the official language of Catalonia. Castilian Spanish is also an official language, as it is the official language of the Spanish state." This issue was heavily debated leading up to the vote on June 18, 2006. One organization, *Seispuntouno* (referring to Article 6.1) argued that both Catalan and Castilian Spanish characterize the multicultural identity of Catalonia. However, the organization, *Seispuntouno*, was founded on the idea that the new Statute attempts to substitute Catalan for Castilian Spanish and thus discriminates against the millions of Catalan citizens whose native language is Castilian Spanish. This is linked to the migration of Spaniards from other parts of Spain during the latter part of the Francoist era for economic reasons. These second and third generation citizens are Castilian Spanish speakers, making language policy in a multicultural and multilingual Catalan population highly complex. The organization, *Seispuntouno*, aimed to substitute the following for Article 6.1:

the languages of Catalan citizens are Catalan and Castilian Spanish. As such, both are the languages of normal and preferred use in public administrations and means of public communication in Catalonia, and they are also the languages normally used as the lingua franca and the languages of instruction.

Arguments were made that with Article 6.1, children from other parts of Spain that have migrated to Catalonia and now live in Catalonia would be discriminated in schools in which Catalan is the language of instruction. I draw on this example to illustrate the cultural and linguistic struggles that underpin debates over autonomy for Catalonia. The struggle over language policy and cultural identity issues continues to shape the political discourse underlying policy production processes.

The political parties of Catalonia were mixed in terms of their positions on the new Statute. The regional parties, PP and the ERC were both opposed to the new Statute, however for very distinct reasons. The PP maintained its patriotic pro-Spain unity position and argued that the new Statute in Catalonia was unconstitutional. The ERC's position, on the other hand, claimed that the Statute was too weak in its stance on deepening Catalan autonomy. The CiU, PSC, and ICV all supported the referendum on the Statute. Each of these political parties, including those opposed, launched large campaigns throughout Catalonia. For example, the CiU's support of the Statute was represented in its 2.2 million dollar campaign that focused on a comparison between Catalonia in 1979 and Catalonia in 2006. Their campaign featured expressions, "1979 or the future?" to express the idea that if the Statute was not approved, Catalonia would "remain chained to 1979" (Gisbert, 2006). Even with the political debates surrounding the Statute, and the expensive campaigns launched by each of Catalonia's political parties, it is worth noting that the participation in the June 18, 2006 vote was remarkably low.

Late on June 18, 2006, President of the Generalitat, Pasqual Maragall publicly announced "*Ja Tenim Estatut*" (We have a Statute) in an institutional declaration. With 73.92% of the voters in support for the Statute over the 20.74% opposition, the referendum on the Statute was passed. However, from data from the June 19, 2006 report in La Vanguardia newspaper (Aroca, 2006), voter participation was low, with votes cast by only 49.4% of the total population in Catalonia. In the 1979 vote on the Statute of Autonomy in Catalonia, 59.3% of the population voted. Even with the low participation, President Maragall and the government in Catalonia interpreted the overwhelming support of the referendum expressed in the vote to be a new era for Catalonia. In Castilian Spanish, as a message to the rest of Spain, he stated,

with the resounding victory of those who voted 'yes' for the referendum, Catalonia will initiate a new stage in its self-government that will be long and positive. It will also be a stage in which Catalonia will feel more comfortable and understood by a plural Spain that is making progress. (Aroca, 2006, p. 17)

Many of the individuals interviewed reflected on the significance of the state for Catalan policy-making, and specifically its impact on Catalonia's educational competencies.

One educational authority stated, "in Catalonia, we have strong social demand for the greatest decentralization and whatever thing facilitates it, I think is positive" (personal communication). This, the educational authority argued, will mean that Catalonia will have more room within the decentralized structure to make an impact in Catalan education policy development. An authority on legal issues in Catalonia outlined the areas in education that specifically are impacted by the Statute. Given the shared competencies, the Spanish Constitution determined that the central state has competencies over anything considered fundamental right. As outlined above, educational governance is shared between Catalonia and the central state. There is a part that is exclusive to the Generalitat, which is considered to fall outside the area covered by fundamental rights guaranteed by the state.

In education, the shared competencies in education between Catalonia and the central state, as dictated by the Spanish Constitution, begin with students at the age of three. The new 2006 Statute of Autonomy has declared governance over early childhood education, from ages zero to three, as an exclusive competency of Catalonia. This has been the biggest impact that the Statute makes in the area of education. Consequently, educational authorities in Catalonia suggested that education policy production would not be affected by the new Statute. One educational authority stated, "the Statute will have no influence whatsoever in education" (personal communication). Others criticized the declaration of early childhood education as exclusive to the Generalitat, and argued that this does not make any real progress on expanding Catalonia's autonomy over education policy formation.

One government official stated that alone, the Statute would not actually permit greater educational competencies for Catalan policy production. Yet, along with other legislative shifts and the current political environment in Spain and Catalonia, shifts could be made that would allow increased room for Catalonia to create its own educational policies. As argued by an educational authority, "now, with the National Pact for Education, the LOE, and the promotion of the Statute, actually we can speak about having a Catalan law of education in which we could have competencies unlike any we have ever had before" (personal communication). The following section looks specifically at a recent policy produced in Catalonia, entitled the National Pact for Education in Catalonia.

THE LOE

In 2006, the Socialist Party introduced a new educational bill, entitled the Organic Law of Education (LOE). The LOE "clarifies the legal framework as it rescinds the three Acts that constituted the basic legislative framework of the whole education system," including the 1990 LOGSE, the 1995 LOPEG, and the 2002 LOCE, and makes some amendments to the 1985 LODE (Eurydice, 2008, p. 72). There are a number of key aims and objectives of the LOE. Overall, the LOE aims to promote fundamental equality of rights and freedoms, democratic notions of peace, human rights, social cohesion, respect and expansion of a multilingual and multicultural Spain (in part through the development of additional foreign languages) and principles of coexistence, solidarity and cooperation. New developments have been around citizenship education, demonstrating the importance placed on citizenship in Spanish education policies for the further development of a democratic, decentralized, Europeanized Spain.

Citizenship Education, with the LOE, is now included as a content area in the 3rd cycle of primary education for the first time in educational legislative history in Spain. While content areas such as "Education for peace" are integrated across different curricular subjects, the LOE mandates the inclusion of "Education for citizenship and human rights" (MEC, 2006, Article 24) within the last cycle of primary education. The LOE also emphasizes citizenship education in secondary education, to be integrated into various content areas. As demonstrated by the LOE, the policy has shifted away from Castilian Spanish nationalism and Catholicism towards an image of Spain as a multi-cultural, democratic, and modern European state. This is shown in the adoption of the "Education for citizenship and human rights" curriculum (MEC, 2006), which originated from a 2002 Council of Europe recommendation. This new curriculum emphasizes the values of the "European ideal citizen" (Engel & Ortloff, 2009).

This push, emanating from the Council of Europe recommendation, moved central-state policy towards a redefinition of the European citizen in citizenship education curriculum. Yet, we need to see this pressure from 'above' the central state in a context of decentralization and fragmentation from 'below', which also pushes for a different perspective on citizenship education. From within the Spanish state, Catalonia has long utilized citizenship education as a means of instilling values of Catalan nationalism, including the promotion of Catalan linguistic and cultural heritage, and the push for greater autonomy from Spain. Yet, in the Catalan case, policy and curriculum also emphasize the supranational as embodying the values of multiculturalism, multilingualism, and democracy. In this way, there is an implication that the supranational legitimizes regional nationalism (Engel, 2007a).

The LOE also sets out several educational aims related to the international dimension of curriculum, such as respect for Spanish linguistic and cultural diversity as an enriching trait of society or education for peace, respect for human rights, social cohesion, co-operation and solidarity among peoples (Eurydice, 2008). Through examining a European Commission country report, which is self-reported by the Spanish central government, we obtain a particular view of the ways in which the Spanish government would like to portray their policy on citizenship education to the outside world.

THE NATIONAL PACT FOR EDUCATION IN CATALONIA

In Catalonia, the Department of Education, along with principal local and regional educational actors in Catalonia, came together on March 20, 2006 to sign the National Pact for Education in Catalonia. Marta Cid, the Education Counselor, led the movement for the National Pact. This document was based on the Generalitat de Catalunya (2005a) document, *Pacte Nacional per a l'Educació oportunitat i compromís: Idees per al debat* (National Pact for educational opportunity and compromise: Ideas for the debate). The 2006 Pact was signed by 18 other organizations: three workers' unions and their teaching federations (USOC, UGT, CC.OO), four representative organizations of private schools (*Agrupació Escolar Catalana, Federació de Centres d'Ensenyament, Fundació Escola Cristiana de Catalunya y Confederació de Centres Autònoms d'Ensenyament*), four parental federations (FAPAC, FAPAES, FAPEL, and la *Federación de padres de alumnos de educación especial*), municipal associations (*Federació de Municipis de Catalunya y Associació Catalana de Municipis i Comarques*), AJEC (the Association of Young Students of Catalonia), APSEC (the Professional Association of Education Services of Catalonia), and the movements of pedagogical renovation and the *Col•legi Oficial de Doctors i Llicenciats en Filosofia i Lletres i en Ciències*. Notably absent from the signing of the National Pact was the Union of Teaching Workers of Catalonia (USTEC), the union that represents public education. The following two sections offer an analysis of two debates over policy production within the National Pact. The first relates to the issue over public and private networks of schools, and the second specifically relates to shifts in decentralization.

Public/Private Divide

The document, *National Pact for Education in Catalonia*, examined what were agreed to be the central educational issues in Catalonia today. These included the overall quality of the education system, pedagogical innovations, guarantees for equality of opportunities, and social cohesion. In Catalonia, a central theme that has shifted the policy focus in education is equity and equality of opportunities. As one educational leader, who was heavily involved in the process of writing and negotiating the National Pact of Education, stated, "the National Pact suggests that above all, we are proposing that we are all in accordance to make education in Catalonia more equal, more equitable, and the guarantee that all students have the right to education" (personal communication). One of the core problems that the Catalan Department of Education seeks to improve is the inequality between public schools and "*centros concertados*," which are schools that are private, but receive state subsidies (Jacott & Maldonado Rico, 2006). From this point on for clarity, I will refer to these schools as semi-private.

The contemporary Spanish educational system is comprised of schools that are considered either public or private, with a sector of semi-private schools that receive public funds to compensate for costs covered in financial agreements between public authorities and private schools that receive state subsidies. Efforts have been made to address this issue and equalize the quality of all Spanish schools. However, as Pereyra (2002) noted, the semi-private sector of education is now more ingrained within contemporary Spanish society, exemplified in the increase in semi-private school enrollments, which in Catalonia is up to 50%. Moreover, these semi-private schools are allowed to select their students, even though they receive state subsidies. As a result, local and regional educational leaders argued that the selection of students divides students along class and race as public schools continue to primarily enroll the lower socio-economic population, including the immigrant student population, while middle and upper class children attend semi-private schools. The National Pact has attempted to alter this phenomenon so that "the educational centers that receive public money cannot select or exclude, and that definitively a citizen can attend whatever school that they like" (personal communication). The National Pact, through a number of educational changes, aims to make these two school networks equitable and equal along the logic of school choice.

One mechanism for achieving the goal of equalizing these multiple school networks is the implementation of a sixth hour in public primary schools across Catalonia. As part of the National Pact, primary school hours will be extended from 25 hours a week to 30 hours a week, with the addition of the sixth hour. The semi-private schools have out-performed the public schools scholastically, for example as measured by the recent PISA evaluation in mathematics (Maset, 2006). Semi-private schools have more annual instruction hours than public schools in Catalonia. Therefore, to equalize the two networks, it was proposed that public schools add on an additional hour to each school day. The sixth hour became one of the contested topics involved in debates over the National Pact. In fact, the inclusion of a sixth hour in the National Pact was essentially what kept USTEC from supporting the National Pact. The position of USTEC held that the sixth hour was not a primary educational issue for public schools. However, the sixth hour was promoted and implemented in order to equalize the calendar and number of hours of instruction between public and semi-private schools (personal communication).

Decentralization

In addition, there was a call for greater participation for the City Councils (*Ayuntamientos*), which represent the local and municipal government in Barcelona. In the process of democratization and decentralization in Spain, it was argued in the National Pact that in Catalonia, decentralization must extend beyond the level of the regional Catalan Department of Education to local and municipal levels. Included in this objective is the idea that with greater autonomy and more resources provided directly to the local levels, educational quality and innovation would vastly improve (Generalitat de Catalunya, 2002b). This would create more democratic participation and aid in creating more equal opportunities. City Councils have also maintained a significant role during the building of the Spanish mass education system. One educational system actor indicated the overall importance of the City Councils in Barcelona, beginning during the implementation of the General Law of Education (LGE) in 1970.

During this time, the state was unable and unwilling to spend the necessary resources to create more schools to meet the demands of a developing mass education system. City Councils essentially filled the gap left by the absence of the Spanish state in education. In Barcelona, an educational leader explained that one City Council had 79 schools that included primary, secondary, and art schools.

This was unusual in Spain for this time due to absence of educational services offered by the state and the Generalitat in Catalonia, the local levels of government in Catalonia began to construct schools and enhance the educational opportunities of Catalan citizens. In the introduction of the National Pact, it has been argued that Catalonia historically has possessed its own educational institutions. As a result, the document states that major advances in education have been made during the pre-Franquist era that create a necessary environment for a current National Pact of Education in Catalonia.

While these changes are just off the ground in Catalonia, many of the individuals interviewed placed their hope in the National Pact for Education as the groundwork for a future educational law produced by Catalonia for Catalonia. In this way, the National Pact represented a base for Catalan education policy production. Along with the approval of the referendum on the Statute, which extended Catalan competencies in a number of areas, as well as a political environment marked by a Socialist government, which has appeared to be more open towards supporting greater autonomy for Catalonia, during this period, there was potential for Catalonia to create a roadway for greater policy-making competencies within the Spanish state. As one policy-maker in Barcelona expressed in 2006, "we are just getting the ideas included in the National Pact off of the ground, and we do not know how far it will take us, but it is work that involves a lot of expectations" (personal communication). These expectations underlie the desire in Catalonia for greater autonomy over areas of education policy production and the pressures that readily inform policy formation processes.

The following chapter extends this discussion through a lens placed specifically on the state's negotiation of European pressures and broader global processes. The next chapter explores Europe and the development of a European education policy space. First, the chapter offers a historical overview of Europe's developing educational priorities from the conception from the 1951 Treaty of Paris to the recent post-Lisbon era. Across these developments, the chapter explores the way in which the EU has become a significant policy actor in education policy debates in its Member State countries, and how it has affected education policy production across regions and nation states of Europe.

GLOBAL PRESSURES AND EU EDUCATIONAL PRIORITIES

Europe is united in its resolve that only by working together can we represent our interests and goals in the world of tomorrow. The European Union is determined to contribute its ideas of a sustainable, efficient and just economic and social order to the global process.
(Council of the European Union, 2007)

The previous chapter examined the changing territorial shape, and shifting political and economic organization of the Spanish state. These changes have resulted in a complex division of educational competencies between the central state and Catalonia. In the development of the mass modern education system in Spain, many of the new policy directives appear to be influenced by global and European pressures (Dale & Robertson, 2002; Morrow & Torres, 2003). As states increasingly work to align their educational systems with the demands of the global economy, IOs and supranational organizations have begun to develop educational programs and have become policy actors in their own right.

In the EU, a European education policy space has been developed in recent decades, according to the EU's particular political, economic, cultural, and social aims (Nóvoa & Lawn, 2002). This chapter begins with a discussion of the EU and then provides a brief historical background to the construction of the EU. Next, this chapter draws on key policy documents in order to trace the development of EU educational interests and priorities since the 1951 Treaty of Paris, as illustrated in the construction of a European education policy space and its significance for Spain and Catalan. In the latter part of this chapter, the focus is on regionalism in the EU, with particular attention given to Catalonia.

PROJECT FOR A NEW EUROPE

As a union of 27 European countries that have committed to work together to pursue common policies in certain areas, originally economic policy, the EU has been called one of the most unique institutional creations of today's world. From a continent divided and punctuated by two devastating world wars, the construction of the EU has become the greatest experiment of European integration. To date, the EU has developed into the single largest economic unit and is the only multinational democracy in the world. The EU also exists as the only international organization with a parliament. The EU is a unique organization in the world as it has some of the functions, features, and powers of a supranational government, yet it is restricted in some ways as to what it can legally do without unanimous consent, like the United Nations (UN).

The study of the EU is no simple undertaking, given the complexity in its institutions and policy-making procedures. In discussions of the EU project and its future developments, many supporters and skeptics alike have used Winston Churchill's 1945 phrase "the United States of Europe," (Mauter, 1998). Likewise, there are comparisons between the EU and the UN. However, the EU is not a federation of states as in the US and member states of the EU are not as tightly bound as the states are in the US. The EU, unlike the US, also does not have a Constitution that applies to society, politics, and the economies of all of the member states. A process to establish a constitution began in the dawn of the new millennium and the "Draft Treaty Establishing a Constitution for Europe" was published in 2003 and agreed upon in 2004 (European Commission, 2004).

However, all individual EU member states did not ratify it to bring it legally into effect, which discussed further in this chapter. The EU is also not an organization of countries whose governments cooperate with one another in the same way that the UN does. The EU has much more legal power over its member states than the UN and represents member states in some contexts, such as the World Trade Organization. Therefore, the EU functions differently than the UN, as members of the UN do not surrender any of their decision-making powers. This means that the UN leadership has no power to make member states comply with directives, whereas the EU's central decision-making institutions have a certain amount of authority.

In the EU, there are currently 27 member states that remain sovereign nation states and possess political authority over the citizens, territory, and politics of their country. However, as part of the EU, they delegate some of their sovereignty over decision-making to the supranational entity (the EU) to derive economic and political strength. Against global competitors, in the late 20th century (the US and Japan), the EU has served to join individual member states and provide them with greater global influence than any of the individual member states could not have had alone. The EU's institutions are constructed by member states, which provide these institutions power to make decisions, by which the member states then comply. This power derives from the treaties that member states sign upon their entrance into the EU, meaning that a series of treaties govern the operations of the Union. To further understand the context and function of the EU, it is important to briefly present a historical overview of the construction of the EU.

Historical Roots

Throughout history, Europe has existed as a war-torn continent. Given its tumultuous history, the emergence of harmony in Europe has seemed highly improbable. As stated by Neal and Barbezat (1998), "to gain a historical perspective on current developments...it makes the most sense to start with World War II, the initial division of Germany, and with it the division of Europe into East and West" (p. 5).

After World War II, the Allies did not consider Germany to be a sovereign state, and they aimed to "dismember Germany, as well as to deindustrialize, de-Nazify, and democratize it" (Neal & Barbezat, 1998, p. 5). As a result, there was a partition of Germany between the US, the Soviet Union, Great Britain, and France, which ultimately divided Europe (Neal & Barbezat, 1998). In the immediate post-World War II era, European leaders unified in their agreement that peace, as well as political and economic stability was to be the European imperative.

Inspired by European leaders such as Robert Schuman and Jean Monnet, both French, it was determined that if countries in the continent could cooperate in various projects to pursue joint goals, destructive warlike conflicts would no longer arise. European leaders also believed that partnership in coal and steel was necessary given their tactical use during times of war, and steel and coal were central in both Germany and France's economies. As a result, these European leaders wanted to bind Germany's main (war-making) industries—coal and steel— to those of France, Italy, the Netherlands, Belgium, and Luxembourg (European Commission, n.d.). Known as the Schuman plan, in 1951 the Treaty of Paris was negotiated, founded, and signed, which developed the European Coal and Steel Community (ECSC). The ECSC's purpose was to bind the steel and coal resources of these six countries together. The Treaty of Paris formally was brought into force in July of 1952, marking the first major step towards the EU of today. It finally expired in 2002, fifty years after it came into force.

In the following years, there were additional joint projects, which increased cooperation among countries on a wide range of issues. The formation of the ECSC eventually led to the institutional evolution of the European Economic Community (EEC), which in turn formed the basis for the construction of the EU (Bale, 2005). The EEC was founded in March of 1957 with the signing of the Treaty of Rome. It entered into force in January of 1958. As part of the Treaty of Rome, the EEC consisted of the same six nation states of the ECSC. As these countries cooperatively moved towards greater economic integration, the EEC had great significance for the establishment of an economically unified Europe.

With the construction of the EEC, the six core member states began to eliminate their trade barriers in order to form a common market. Additionally, the Treaty of Rome was significant for its formation of the European institutions, which materialized as the Commission, Council of Ministers, and European Parliament with the 1967 Merger Treaty. The Merger Treaty actively united the six countries, merging the EEC, the European Atomic Energy Community (known as EURATOM, signed also in March of 1957), and the ECSC. From this point on, the merger of these three bodies became known as the European Community (EC), the backbone of the EU today.

With the backdrop of the ECSC, the EEC, and the establishment of these European institutional bodies, two major events of the 1980s and 90s helped construct the contemporary entity of the EU. First, the Single European Act of 1986 "formally brought [European Political Cooperation] together with the [European Community] under the 'single' framework of the European Council" (Forster & Wallace, 2000, p. 465). Second, in 1992, the Treaty on European Union in

Maastricht was signed (negotiations began in 1991) by the Heads of State of EC Member states. The treaty entered into force in November of 1993. This treaty is also commonly referred to as the Maastricht Treaty. This treaty marked the creation of the EU and aimed for closer economic and political cooperation between Member State countries. The Maastricht Treaty changed the title of the European Community to the European Union (EU). This change in title is thought to reflect a realization that with the increasing number of Member states, integration had to extend beyond an economic union to involve more of a social, political, and cultural focus (Dale & Robertson, 2002).

The Maastricht Treaty constructed the three pillars of intergovernmental partnership in the EU, which include Economic Integration, Common Security and Foreign Policy, and Community Justice and Home Rule system. Furthermore, the Maastricht Treaty created two landmark economic arrangements that have countered all arguments that economic and political cooperation among European nation states was improbable. The EU first continued along its mission of breaking down trade barriers across its member states and created what today is considered the common European market. Along with the common market, the economic and monetary union (EMU) was constructed. This involved that creation of a single currency, the euro, which is managed by the European Central Bank, which sets interest rates and controls money supply. The euro has replaced 16 of the EU member state's currencies, jointly known as the eurozone, with more countries to join in the future.

In addition, emphasis was placed on increasing mobility of citizens of EU member states and the breakdown of EU borders. As a result of the Schengen Agreement, internal border controls of select EU countries have been removed in hopes of enhancing mobility among European countries. Many EU member states, as well as non-EU member states, such as Iceland and Norway, participate in the Schengen Agreement, although Ireland and the UK are partial members with their border controls maintained. Increased mobility across EU and other European countries is thought to be essential and desirable for greater economic development.

It is important to note that while efforts have increased to continue eroding the EU's internal borders, its external borders have remained highly monitored, and have existed as a major challenge to EU governance. In 2006, news from Spain's autonomous cities of Ceuta and Melilla in northern Africa and issues of immigration within Spain and the EU suggest the complexity surrounding the notions of open mobility within the EU. In a comparative paper focused on citizenship education and immigration in Bavaria and Catalonia, it was argued that

> the boundary between the familiar and the foreign is occasionally expanded to the European level but it is still maintained. One might develop a sense of being part of the European community in terms of the currency and travel without constraints across borders, but borders are maintained when it comes to unwanted African immigrants who try to enter on boats. Moreover, when considering the changes in citizenship and immigration laws and how they have invoked a negative sense of multiculturalism internally in the political

rhetoric, it appears or is implied that diversity is acceptable at the European level—but only in regard to European 'natives' and not to immigrants. (Engel & Ortloff, 2009, p. 194)

Although highly desirable for Europe's economic development, concepts of open mobility and multiculturalism appear quite weak.

In addition, the Maastricht Treaty represents the creation of a distinct institutional system of the EU. The EU is made up of three main decision-making institutions: the European Commission, European Council, and the European Parliament (cf. Bale, 2005). The European Commission consists of one commissioner from each EU member country, who is responsible for a particular policy. The Commission proposes new laws for the EU, and then sends their proposal to the European Parliament and the Council of the European Union. The European Parliament is the only organ of the EU that is directly elected by citizens of the EU. The Parliament's chief responsibility is to discuss new laws being proposed by the European Commission.

If the Parliament does not approve a proposal, it can ask the Commission to change it until the Parliament is satisfied that this is a good law. This is called the Codecision II procedure. Overall, the predominant role of the European Parliament is advisory. The Council of the European Union also plays an important role in developing new EU laws. Each law has to be discussed by government ministers from all of the EU countries. The Council's members include one minister from each EU country. After discussing a proposal, the Council votes on it. There are rules about how many votes each country has, and how many are needed to pass a law. In some cases, the rule says the Council has to be in complete agreement. Once the Council and the Parliament have passed a new law, EU governments have to ensure that it is respected in their countries.

For the purposes of this book, there are two other governing bodies that are worth mentioning: the European Economic and Social Committee and the Committee of the Regions (COR). The European Economic and Social Committee is the bridge between the EU and civil society. It is a formal platform for citizens and economic and social interest groups to voice their opinions on EU matters. It has an advisory role in that its opinions are sent to the larger institutions of the EU. The COR also has an advisory role in issues of EU policy-making: it "advises (though it cannot compel) other EU institutions on policy and legislation that affect local and regional government" (Bale, 2005, p. 46). The COR is considered to be the voice of local and regional governments in Europe as it represents both local and regional authorities. The COR is consulted prior to EU decisions on issues, such as regional and local policy, the environment, education, and transport. The significance of the COR for Catalonia is discussed further below.

Enlargement

The process of European integration with the Maastricht Treaty was impelled largely by a goal of strengthening the European economy through combining countries' resources. This process continues today, and is one of the continuing motivations for EU enlargement. The EU has grown from the original six to 27 members, with more countries preparing to join. From the original six members of France, Germany, Italy, the Netherlands, Belgium, and Luxembourg, 21 new states have joined over the course of 30 years. To attain EU membership, there are a number of criteria that a country has to meet to become a candidate for accession into the EU, and subsequently become a EU Member State.

The 1993 the Copenhagen European Council established criteria that each candidate country must achieve:
– Stability of institutions guaranteeing democracy, the rule of law, human rights and respect for and protection of minorities;
– The existence of a functioning market economy as well as the capacity to cope with competitive pressure and market forces within the Union;
– The ability to take on the obligations of membership including adherence to the aims of political, economic & monetary union (European Commission, 1983, Copenhagen European Council Section).

Therefore, there are political and economic criteria, as well as additional obligations to adhere to and implement all European legislation. The economic criteria are notable in Spain's accession into the EU in 1986, in which Spain radically revised its economic system. Of the changes in the Spanish system, it had altered its economic policy through a privatization agenda to cut back on public expenditure.

In 1995, the Madrid European Council created additional criteria for candidate countries to meet. The Madrid European Council decided that each candidate country must create the "conditions for its integration through the adjustment of its administrative structures" (European Commission, 1983, Madrid European Council Section). The process for EU membership is lengthy, and involves a number of steps. It begins with the pre-accession strategy that prepares candidate countries and includes a number of negotiations to screen their capabilities to meet the criteria for membership. As the candidate country continues to make progress in a number of economic and political areas for membership, there is an ongoing process of evaluation. Upon completion of this stage, the results are written up in a draft of an Accession Treaty, which is submitted to the European Commission and later to the European Parliament.

The last stage includes the Accession Treaty being submitted to the Member states and the candidate country for their own ratification, followed by the candidate country reaching its official status as a Member State country of the EU. In recent years, the EU has been dramatically enlarged to its current membership of 27 Member State countries. In 2003, the Treaty of Accession was unanimously supported, which accepted 10 out of the 13 accession countries that applied for EU membership. Most recently, Bulgaria and Romania have joined in January of 2007 and Croatia, the former Yugoslav Republic of Macedonia, and Turkey are now considered candidates for EU membership. Albania and Montenegro are currently in a stage of negotiation as potential candidate countries. There still involves tension surrounding Turkey's entrance into the EU, as well as challenges emerging from the recent global economic crisis.

Constitution

In 2004, the "Draft Treaty Establishing a Constitution for Europe" (European Commission, 2004) was agreed upon as a necessary step for European integration, in order "to provide a single document to replace the various treaties (Rome, the draft SEA, Maastricht, Amsterdam, Nice, etc.) that over time have laid down how the EU is to be governed" (Bale, 2005, p. 53). The European Constitution does not replace the Constitutions that already exist in most European countries, but it aims to coexist with these Constitutions. This is based on Article I-5.1 of the EU Constitution which stated, "the union shall respect the equality of member states before the Constitution as well as their national identities, inherent in their fundamental structures, political and constitutional" (European Commission, 2004). On October 29, 2004, the Heads of State of the 25 member states and the three candidate countries signed the Treaty establishing a Constitution for Europe, which was unanimously adopted by them on June 18, 2004.

The Constitution worked to position the values, rights, and responsibilities of the EU and its member states. Article I-1.1 stated that the "Constitution establishes the European Union, on which the member states confer competences to attain objectives they have in common. The Union shall coordinate the policies by which the member states aim to achieve these objectives" (European Commission, 2004). The Constitution indicated a number of values, including "values of respect for human dignity, freedom, democracy, equality, the rule of law and respect for human rights, including the rights of persons belonging to minorities," and societal values are those of "pluralism, non-discrimination, tolerance, justice, solidarity and equality between women and men" (European Commission, 2004, Article I-2). Additionally, Title I Articles relate to the creation of an open market in the EU, in which mobility of citizens, goods, and capital is guaranteed.

However, the ratification of any EU Treaty can only take place with a vote in each of the member states. In other words, it only takes one member state to vote against a treaty for the treaty to not be ratified. Debates surrounding the EU Constitution varied greatly in each member state country, and ranged from tensions over the construction of a European suprastate, criticisms that even with a Constitution, the EU would continue to remain too distant from its citizens, and appraisal of the Constitution as a necessary step to ensure democratization and peace in the region, and one which would further the political, economic, social, and cultural integration of Europe. During the ratification process, the citizens of France and the Netherlands rejected the text of the Constitution on 29 May and 1 June of 2005 respectively. A two-year period of reflection, discussion, or what Bresso (2006) argued was more of a period of uncertainty immediately followed in all EU countries.

Lisbon Strategy

One of the important recent institutional and policy developments in the EU has been the Lisbon Strategy. In 2000, the Lisbon Strategy (also known as the Lisbon Agenda) was launched, which aimed to create "the most dynamic and competitive knowledge-based economy in the world capable of sustainable economic growth with more and better jobs and greater social cohesion" by 2010 (European Commission, 2000). The strategy was supported by three primary pillars: economic, social and environmental. A number of targets and benchmarks were set as well in order to achieve the Lisbon Strategy, including the reliance on indicators and benchmarks, such as through the Open Method of Coordination (OMC), to measure progress. The use of indicators and the OMC is discussed further in this chapter.

In 2003, in different policy areas, a general consensus began to emerge that the EU would not meet the goals set out by the Lisbon Strategy and that urgent reforms were necessary. In the following year, a High Level Group chaired by Wim Kok was established and from this group, a 2004 report, *Facing the Challenge* was published. This report indicated that not only would Europe fall short of meeting the Lisbon Strategy goals, but since its launch in 2000, the gap in growth between Europe and its competitors (North America and Asia) had expanded (High Level Group, 2004). As reported by Robertson (2007), the High Level Group's report exuded a "crisis discourse."

Holford (2008) wrote that there were major political challenges surrounding or underlying the "crisis" period of the Lisbon Strategy. Of these challenges, one of the major issues at the time was the accession of "new member states from central and eastern Europe, with very different political and cultural histories, and traditions of citizenship and democracy, significantly extended the range of inequality of income and wealth among the Union's population" (Holford, 2008, p. 334). Another one of the major challenges at the time had to do with political legitimacy, which "were thrown sharply into focus when referenda on the European Constitution in France and the Netherlands demonstrated a deep level of disenchantment with the European project in member states not previously through highly 'Eurosceptical'" (Holford, p. 12).

After the period of reflection following the failure to ratify the European Constitution, in 2007, EU leaders agreed to push forward a new Reform Treaty by the end of the year. At the end of 2007, the final text of the Treaty was adopted and the 27 member state countries signed the Treaty of Lisbon in December 2007. The Treaty of Lisbon has been intended to respond to the new challenges presented to an enlarged EU, such as those emanating from globalization and increased mobility. Therefore, to meet the twin goals of the EU, which are economic development and social cohesion, the amended Lisbon Agenda looks to meet these challenges and demands through the following changes: a more democratic and transparent Europe, a more efficient Europe, a Europe of rights and values, freedom, solidarity and security, and Europe as an actor on the global stage (European Commission, n.d.).

Significance for Catalonia

Both the enlargement of the EU and the EU Constitution debates has been important for Catalonia. In chapter 3, I traced the development of pressures facing Spain during the post-Francoist era and the link drawn between modernization and

Europeanization. The "symbolic attachment to the ideal of Europe" as a means to modernizing Spain has continued even after joining the EC (Moravcsik, 1998, p. 41). For example, in the 2004 ratification of the EU Constitution, Spaniards voters overwhelmingly supported the Constitution and called themselves "the most grateful Europeans." For Catalonia, the vote on the EU Constitution became a political dilemma over the place of Catalonia with the EU context, and the extent to which the EU was fulfilling Catalonia's particular nationalist aims. Guibernau (2006) argued that for many Catalan citizens,

> who are used to turning to Europe as a model of democracy, progressivism, cultural and artistic movements and socio-economic progress—is whether they can vote 'no' to the EU Constitution while maintaining a strong commitment to Europe or whether, on the other hand, they should say 'yes' to a Constitution that does not satisfy their aspirations. (p. 220)

For Catalan voters, the recognition of the Catalan language as an official language of the EU was a central consideration.

Moreover, the enlargement from 15 to 25 Member State countries in 2003 also became a highly political issue for Catalonia and the other CCAA of Spain, as there was a concern regarding EU funding for less economically advantaged regions and anxiety over immigration. From what was once a small EU state to what is now considered the ninth largest economy in the world, according to IMF (2009) GDP figures for 2008, the enlargement debates show the remarkable shifts that have occurred in Spain over the past several decades.

Concrete steps have been taken towards the construction of economic and political stability in Europe. However, these issues for Catalonia represent several examples of the challenges that face the continued development of the EU project. The experiment for European integration has pressed the EU towards its contemporary status of one of the most powerful global players. As the EU has continued to develop, education has become a focal point linked to global economic competition and culturally, the further creation of a unified Europe. The following section traces the development of EU interests and priorities for education policy production, shown in the construction of a European education policy space.

CONSTRUCTING A EUROPEAN EDUCATION POLICY SPACE

Education is often regarded as a crucial piece in the larger European integration project of, to borrow Morely and Robins' (1995) expression, "'unity in diversity' of European culture" (p. 3). It is widely held that the vision of European economic revitalization and social cohesion must develop politically, culturally, economically, socially, and educationally. Carrajo (1993) argued that "cooperation among the EC member states in educational matters is a part of th[e] logic of building a united Europe, since it tends to bring people closer and to improve their living and working conditions" (p. 179). In these efforts, a European education policy space has been constructed and in recent years, expanded (cf. Lawn & Lingard, 2002).

In the economic, political, social, and cultural development of the EU, education has played a significant role. As a result, processes of education policy production in regions and nation states of the EU have been subsequently reshaped in a number of directions. While it is commonly understood that the Maastricht Treaty of the early 1990s clearly pushed education into an area of EU competency, "in order to understand what is presently happening in the field of co-operation in education on a European level, a minimum of reference to the historical development is necessary" (Hingel, 2001, p. 4). In order to map out a broad history, I draw on four historical periods outlined in Hingel's (2001) report between 1971 and 2000, also including education in the context of the 1957 Treaty of Rome into the framework as well.

In the 1950s, education was a "taboo subject" in European discourse and debates, and therefore not included in the Treaty of Rome (Blitz, 2003, p. 4). In the 1957 Treaty of Rome, the focus on education was predominantly on vocational training. This is related to the overarching attention on economic restoration from World War II. With the emergence of the idea of an internal European market emerged, an interest in the education of EEC countries began to develop, and with the project for a more integrated Europe, education for means of cultural cohesion among EU citizens also became a focus for the EEC. As early as the 1970s, "a cultural and education strategy was produced which would begin the task of constructing Europe as a common space, and the role of education in this task was seen as a necessary step" (Nóvoa & Lawn, 2002, p. 2). During the 1970s, there were concrete steps taken in the area of education by the Ministers of Education of the original six countries.

In 1971, the six Ministers of Education held their first meeting and cooperatively worked to establish two working groups for future work in education (Hingel, 2001). In 1976, the first resolution was agreed to, which established "an 'action programme' which included mainly, studies, research, visits, compilation of up-to-date documentation and statistics in a number of educational fields" (Hingel, 2001, p. 5). The conceptualization of education was aligned with a "social and public investment in current and future workers that [would] potentially secure social cohesion and social stability" (Dale & Robertson, 2002, p. 24–25). Even within this social perspective, Dale and Robertson (2002) argued, interests in education remained largely focused on human capital formation.

In the decades that followed, education became an increasingly important area of work for the EC. Education in the EC often was looked at as the solution to economic problems, including the construction of a more competitive workforce through human capital development. Karlsen (2002) stated, "education and training are the answers to the main problems in the Community" (p. 26). Economic interests in education also remained central, particularly in relation to global competition both from the US and Japan during the 1980s. Karlsen (2002) has written about four areas of education that were developed in order to meet the economic and political goals set by the EC in the 1980s and early 1990s. The first dealt directly with vocational training programs to "cover post-secondary education, and the intention was to strengthen the vocational relevance and the practical economic application of post-secondary education" (p. 28). The second area of educational programs related to providing opportunities for greater mobility of teachers and students to other educational institutions in Europe. These programs included Erasmus, Lingua, and Youth for Europe (Karlsen, 2002). Erasmus, established in 1987 under the EU's lifelong learning program, aims at increased mobility among higher education students. Lingua is a program that provides emphasis on linguistic diversity in the EU, aims to enhance the quality in teaching and learning of languages, and promote greater access to lifelong language learning opportunities. Youth for Europe was a program launched to increase the mobility of groups of young people.

The third area of educational programs emphasized "compensatory actions and support for better opportunities for marginal groups and regions," including a focus on women, the disabled, and regional programs in Central and Eastern Europe (p. 28). Lastly, Karlsen (2002) discussed the fourth area, which focused on the development of programs, such as Eurydice, that collected and disseminated data and information on the educational systems in Europe. This last area aligns with Hingel's (2001) report, in which he stated that educational systems of Member State countries have had an important role in the "mutual trust-building process (between the Member states, as well as between the Member states and the Commission)" and that the "Eurydice collection and analysis of data and information, in close co-operation with Eurostat, has been primordial" (p. 6). With the Maastricht Treaty, education became a significant area of interest given its potential for social cohesion and human capital (Hingel, 2001).

With the 1992 Maastricht Treaty, education was launched into a new domain of EU legislation and competencies. In the Treaty, "'education' was formally recognized as a major responsibility of the EU and not just the Member states" (Nóvoa & Lawn, 2002, p. 3). However, the principle of subsidiarity, meaning that EU decision-making must be carried out at the closest level to the citizen, was central to the determination of the EU's role in the educational systems of its Member states. This is indicated in Article 126 of the Maastricht Treaty. Article 126.1 (now Article 149.1) stated that

> the Community shall contribute to the development of quality education by encouraging cooperation between Member states and, if necessary, by supporting and supplementing their action, while fully respecting the responsibility of the Member states for the content of teaching and the organization of education systems and their cultural and linguistic diversity. (European Commission, 1992).

However vague and ambiguous the principle of subsidiarity, as Hingel (2001) stated, "education is an ideal-type of policy area for subsidiarity to play its full role" (p. 3). This is because education has historically played such a key role in nation state building, and nation states are protective of their national systems of education.

The 1990s proved to be a significant era of educational development in the EU. In 1994, a European Commission White Paper entitled *Growth, Competitiveness, Employment* was published, which outlined education as a solution to problems in these three areas: growth, competitiveness, and employment (European Commission, 1994). In addition, during the 1990s, two programs were launched to expand mobility and cooperation between students and teachers: Leonardo da Vinci, which focused on vocational education, and Socrates, which was geared towards all non-higher educational levels. Karlsen (2002) argued that these "two restructured education programmes based on a new legal foundation in the Treaty of Maastricht, marked the end of a long period where education had a marginal and obscure status in Community policy" (p. 35). In the last half of the 1990s, new policy initiatives were launched by the European Commission. These included "three major trends: internationalisation of trade, information society and new technology and growth in scientific knowledge" (Karlsen, 2002, p. 36). The 1996 *White Paper, Teaching and Learning—Towards the Learning Society*, outlined a series of central objectives, such as the acquisition of new knowledge, the cooperation of educational and business sectors, the fight against exclusion, proficiency in multiple languages, and the treatment of capital investment and investment in training on an equal basis (European Commission, 1996).

In the latter half of the 1990s, education was thought to be the answer in the fight against unemployment in the EU, one of its biggest challenges for Europe at this time. Hingel (2001) stated that the period between 1997 and 1999, "major advancements were made in order for education and training to play its full and central role in policies of especially social cohesion and employment" (p. 7). Hingel (2001) described the launch of the European Employment Strategy, which was "built on four main pillars: employability, entrepreneurship, adaptability and equal opportunities, and it fully included the education and training dimension from the very start" (p. 7). At the turn of the 21st century, the EU was focused on increasing the economic competitiveness of the EU and improving the high rates of unemployment.

In 2000, with the launch of the Lisbon Strategy, education was pushed "forward into a lifelong learning zone, an educational space, and a place for quality education" (Nóvoa & Lawn, 2002, p. 3). With the Lisbon objective, as Hingel (2001) argued, "education policies are here again at the centre of attention of two central messages by way of: an introduction in the conclusions of specific educational benchmarks and guidelines, and the invitation to Ministers of Education to reflect on Common objectives for educational systems in Europe" (p. 14). Hingel (2001) went on to argue that in no other policy areas in Europe are the conclusions as explicitly stated than in the Lisbon conclusions.

The predominant emphasis placed on education during the period immediately after the Lisbon objective was to facilitate lifelong learning, assume sound methods of quality assurance, and above all, aid in the development of a knowledge-based economy. The EU has been prominent in pushing forward the idea of the knowledge economy and lifelong learning, both of which have generated expansive literature in the area of education. Karlsen (2002) outlined the "European Educational Area," including the following elements: "knowledge, continually expanding and renewing in a life-long learning process, enhancement of citizenship through sharing common values and a sense of belonging to the EU as a common social and cultural entity"

(p. 38). The EU, in the development of a European model of education, has steadily promoted the view of education as both a means for greater human capital and competitive labor force, as well as social cohesion.

These underlying educational values were reflected in the draft of the European Constitution. First, in the Constitution, Article I-3 laid out the Union's objectives. Article 1-3.3 stated that the aims of the EU included

> balanced economic growth and price stability, a highly competitive social market economy, aiming at full employment and social progress, and a high level of protection and improvement of the quality of the environment. It shall combat social exclusion and discrimination, and shall promote social justice and protection, equality between women and men, solidarity between generations and protection of the rights of the child. It shall promote economic, social and territorial cohesion, and solidarity among Member states. (European Commission, 2004)

While education was not specifically mentioned, I want to highlight the focus of these objectives as both geared towards social cohesion and economic growth. In Title III of the Constitution, the competencies of the EU and its Member states were developed. Education was specifically mentioned in the Constitution under Article I-17 Areas of supporting, coordinating or complementary action. It stated that the EU "shall have competence to carry out supporting, coordinating or complementary action...at [the] European level...education, youth, sport and vocational training" (European Commission, 2004). Other areas under this umbrella included health, industry, culture, tourism, civil protection, and administrative cooperation.

Due to the complementary role that the EU has constructed for itself in terms of its own role and power over education, interviews with national and regional policy-makers in Spain and Catalonia seems to reflect that the EU has had little to no effect on education policy in Member states, and that education policy has been left largely up to Member states. One educational leader in Spain stated that the EU has had no influence on education policy production in Spain because it is "the one thing that is rigidly protected by the Spanish government" (personal communication). Another educational leader stated that "apart from the higher education system, where the Bologna Process is happening, I do not see anything that indicates that Europe has any influence" in education (personal communication). One government official stated, "the EU just develops objectives" (personal communication), arguing that the EU's role in education was to jointly develop objectives with Ministers of Education in member states.

Most of the government officials and policy-makers perceived and reflected on education policy in terms of educational legislation or national policy and practice, reflecting on a lack of a specific EU role in education. Education, in their view, is a sensitive area for EU governance. Yet, there appears to be a distinction to be made between policy discourses and practice. As one government official in Madrid stated, "the EU does not have any influence because the policy-makers do not change things but the policy-makers know about it and speak about it frequently at conferences, seminars, meetings" (personal communication). The government official went on to reflect, "if we are talking about the social impact, or the actual changes happening in schools, [the EU] is not changing the school, but it is in the consciousness of policy-makers...this is evident in the many conversations and the discourse" (personal communication). In many interviews, individuals often restated the significance of the principle of subsidiarity in education. This point supports Nóvoa and Lawn's (2002) significant contribution to the literature on educational governance in Europe and the emerging space for European educational interests. They argued that in analyses of education and the EU

> education is viewed in EU-based policy analyses as a minor area of policy, much less significant than the key areas of integration and trade, like law and economic studies. But from a cultural point of view, which recognizes the major shifts and problems of transnational governance, education has a new prominence as the arena in which identity and legitimacy can be created. (p. 4)

In an analysis of the perceptions, beliefs and experiences of participants, education appeared to be a rather insignificant policy area in the EU.

However, in the EU, numerous policy networks have continued to emerge, resulting in the dramatic rescaling the state and regional governance in education. The policy networks include the "formation of new European identities...leading to the emergence of the European education space" (Nóvoa & Lawn, 2002, p. 4). Moreover, Hingel (2001) argued that after the Lisbon declaration that "not only is a European Space of Education in its making, [but] common principles of education are being agreed upon between Member states, leading logically to a European Model of Education" (p. 4). In order to understand the nature of the EU's impact on education, it is helpful to draw on Dale and Robertson's (2002) three power dimensions of EU educational interests.

First, the EU constructs binding decisions among its Member states based on EU membership. Second, members and candidate countries have to abide by particular agendas that the EU establishes. Third, the EU ultimately determines the rules of EU membership, even in "the ways it divides up sectoral responsibilities, and the sticks and carrots it provides to follow particular programs" (p. 27). Consequently, the EU has developed into a powerful actor, with the potential to influence education policy production within its Member states.

Following the framework established in chapter 2, I maintain that the development of multiscalar governance has resulted in a more complex process of policy production, including various actors and numerous pressures across EU, national, regional, and local levels. This aligns with Nóvoa and Lawn's (2002) description of the formation of a European education policy space as an emergent network of a highly complex, overlapping, multilevel set of actors. In this case, in order to understand the significance of EU policy priorities and their impact on education policy, policy has to be seen as a process that involves the construction of new sociospatial entities and cultural spaces across these various scales, including the EU. With these spaces, hard law has moved into "soft stuff" (Holford, 2008) and new policy instruments have been developed.

NEW POLICY INSTRUMENTS AND SOFT GOVERNANCE

While education still operates under the principle of subsidiarity, the EU has developed new education policy instruments aimed to consolidate member state education systems. These new policy instruments have been part of the shift from hard government to soft governance in education (Lawn, 2002). As an offspring of the Lisbon process, the Open Method of Coordination (OMC) is a new policy instrument directed towards the development of cross-national performance benchmarks and standard objectives (Borrás & Jacobsson, 2004; Dale, 2004; Lodge, 2005; Radaelli, 2003; Schäfer, 2006). Particularly in an area like education, in which the principle of subsidiarity outlines a number of boundaries around governance issues, the EU is prevented from advocating a strong agenda. To circumvent this, the OMC was developed as means of cross-national policy coordination under the guise of the development of best practice. In 1998, the EU proposed a working group of national experts to create a set of indicators or benchmarks to further develop standards for evaluation of school systems in member states. Their identification of common educational indicators led to the promotion of the OMC as a new framework for comparison and consolidation of education policy.

Dale (2004) highlighted two views of the OMC. The first is the "OMC as governance" perspective, in which the OMC is "essentially a means of redressing the shortfall in the governance capacity of the EU" (p. 177). This perspective sees the OMC as a new approach to diversity and subsidiarity, in which "mutual cooperation and standard-setting" are highlighted (Dale, p. 178). The OMC's essential purpose has been aligned with the goals of the Lisbon agenda, as its "component parts—benchmarking, indicators, best practice, monitoring and so on—are judged on the basis of their effectiveness as mechanisms for achieving the goals set at Lisbon" (Dale, p. 178). The second perspective of the OMC relates to governmentality.

The OMC, analyzed through a view of governmentality, highlights the process rather than the outcomes. It "focuses more closely on the wider 'Europeanizing' consequences of the processes through which the OMC operates than on their intended outcomes" (Dale, 2004, p. 177). OMC has typically been regarded as "soft law" (Trubek & Trubek, 2005). However, as Radaelli (2003) argued, the OMC has "provide[d] a community of policy-makers with a common vocabulary and a legitimising project" (p. 7). As the OMC constructs a distinctive space of European governance, it also represents the expansion of the European agenda for education and the development of transnational policy networks.

In education, the OMC gathers the best practices to design a set of common objectives for national education systems of member states. Based on the objectives, represented European nation states compile and agree on a set of targeted yardsticks (statistics, indicators) for reaching the set objectives. The process of implementation of these policies remains under the power of each Member State (so not to undermine the principle of subsidiarity). Yet, governments of EU Member states are pressured to align their policies with the OMC's common objectives. Borrás and Jacobsson (2004) wrote, "at face value, the OMC is a collection of mechanisms previously developed under the broad 'soft law' tradition in the EU, such as collective recommendations, review and monitoring, and benchmarking, which also bear similarities with the [OECD]" (p. 188). Similarly, as Larsson (2002) argued, "the dynamics of this [the OMC] have significant implications for national agenda setting. By identifying and making public best practice and by issuing recommendations to individual Member states the Commission and the Council can exert considerable pressure" (p. 13). According to the European Commission (2002),

> the term 'benchmark' is used to refer to concrete, measurable targets. These are grouped into six areas: investment in education and training; early school leavers; graduates in mathematics, science and technology; population having completed upper secondary education; key competencies; lifelong learning. (European Commission, 2007, para. 1)

A 2007 European Commission document revised and established a set of benchmarks and indicators. The document stated that

> indicators and benchmarks are key elements of evidence-based policy making and the monitoring of progress essential to the Lisbon process. They provide the tools for: Statistical underpinning of key policy messages; Analysing progress towards Lisbon objectives, both at the EU and national levels; Identifying examples of good performance which could be subject to peer review and exchange; Comparing EU performance with that of third countries, such as the US and Japan. (European Commission, 2007, p. 1).

In the introduction of the document, the Commission discussed the Education & Training 2010 program.

Here, Ministers of Education of all EU Member states agreed to adopt a set of common educational objectives in alignment with the Lisbon Strategy. These changes are implemented through the OMC, in which "indicators and benchmarks play an important monitoring role and provide support to the exchange of experiences and good practices" (European Commission, 2007, p. 2). Through the establishment of "soft law" (benchmarks, indicators, best practices), the EU, along with other IOs such as the OECD, have influenced education policy production within Member State systems (Trubek & Trubek, 2005). In reflection of these new developments in education, critics have argued that the OMC has become a mechanism through which to promote the EU's agenda, particularly in the OMC's construction of standard European objectives and benchmarks. One of the more critical perspective on the OMC has stemmed from Nóvoa and Yariv-Mashal's (2003) work, in which they argued that "'benchmarking practices' offer a way to achieve co-ordination without '*apparent*' threat to national sovereignty" (p. 429).

Many of the OMC's directives are linked to the Lisbon objective in 2000, and the recent developments in the post-Lisbon era. As the EU attempts to create a more powerful, expansive system of education geared towards greater economic growth and integration, the OMC has become a central policy instrument in which to move in this direction without circumventing the principle of subsidiarity. The point that needs to be emphasized is the overarching significance of the Lisbon strategy in education policy production processes. One educational leader in Catalonia argued that in education "everything that we do, the objective is this one. We want a strong Europe" (personal communication). This participant went on to contrast this goal in light of the interests extending across various scales that now inform education policy production processes: "everyday life is more complicated because we also want a strong Catalonia" and "there is a difficult balance between these two objectives: a strong Europe but a strong region and a strong state" (personal communication). In the aim to extend beyond the Europe-nation state frameworks (e.g. Europe vs. Spain), the next section explores the internationalization and Europeanization of new education policy directives in Catalonia and Spain, prior to moving to the final section of the chapter, which focuses on the intersection of regional, nation state and European policy arenas.

Europeanization of education policy in Spain

Policy-makers and other system actors in Barcelona and Madrid referred to the OMC in much of the same way as international assessments of educational achievement, such as the OECD's PISA. PISA, which aims to compare 15-year old students' scholastic performance across national educational systems, appears to have made a major impact on Catalan policy-makers, government officials, and the general public (Martín, 2006). These developments are reflected in the 2006 Law of Education (LOE) in Spain. An excerpt of the Preamble of the LOE stated that,

> the historic interest in education has been reinforced by the appearance of contemporary educational systems. Those structures dedicated to the formation of the citizen were conceived as fundamental instruments for the construction of nation-states, in the decisive epoch of the configuration of the nation-state. Since then, all countries have paid increasing attention to their educational systems, with the objective of making changes to them according to the changing circumstances and expectations in each historical moment. (MEC, 2006, para. 3)

The Preamble of the LOE stated that due to Spain's accession into the EU, and participation in projects and conferences with other nation states organized by UNESCO, OECD, and other IOs, Spain must now focus on improving upon the quality and effectiveness of its educational system. López (2006) argued that the LOE, in its aim for "quality education for all," establishes these three principles: quality for all, shared effort, and integration in Europe (p. 14). The third principle is described in the Preamble as the goal to adequately prepare Spanish students for the demands of the knowledge economy and open its education system up to the world, including the strive to increase multilingualism among students, increase mobility in the EU, and continue to reform its cooperation with Europe.

This includes a plan for using European benchmarks to determine Spanish educational progress in comparison with other EU Member states. International performance indicators and benchmarks generated from the PISA data have been highly influential in shaping educational reform debates in Spain (Generalitat de Catalunya, 2004). The LOE also represents an overarching goal of consolidating the European dimension of education in Spanish curriculum, through the promotion of knowledge of the EU, education for citizenship in a multicultural society, and teaching of European languages (Ryba, 1993). Educators, administrators, and parents debated the effects of this effort to Europeanize Spanish education, labeled as nothing more than "PR-olicy" (Public Relations Policy) (Lugg, 1997). However, policy-makers, politicians, and Ministers of Education have stated that recent policy has been moving more strongly in the direction towards greater Europeanization of education. Recent research also seems to suggest that Spanish curricular reform has begun to reflect a European dimension and changing notions of democratic citizenship in the context of EU and global processes (De la Caba Collado & López Atxurra, 1996).

As discussed in Engel & Ortloff (2009), Spain's country report (2007-08) for the European Commission Eurybase project continually emphasized a European dimension within the new LOE (2006) and new curriculum in Spain and its regions. As stated in the report, "curricula must include specific measures promoting both the European dimension of education and encouraging the participation of all students and prospective teachers in the different European program" (Eurydice, 2008, p. 14). The LOE (2006) also set out a number of different educational aims that related to global and European dimensions of Spanish curriculum. These included emphasis on respect for Spanish linguistic and cultural diversity as an enriching trait of society and education for peace, respect for human rights, social cohesion, co-operation, and solidarity among peoples here (Eurydice, 2008).

Spain's country report (2007-08) for the European Commission has been self-reported by the central Spanish state and therefore, represents how the Spanish central state would like to portray their educational system and curriculum in a European context (Engel & Ortloff, 2009). Different areas of the Spanish curriculum represent a European and international dimension of education. In primary education, for example, some of the core areas of the curriculum, which include a European dimension are Spanish language and literature and "natural, social and cultural environment" (Eurydice, 2005, p. 5). The earlier country report for Spain (2004-05) stated,

> one of the aims of 'Natural, social and cultural environment' is to develop the identification of students with their social groups of reference and roots, so that from the family and the school they may identify with broader and more abstract groups, such as the Autonomous Community, Spain and the EU, and finally humanity as a whole. (Eurydice, 2005, p. 10)

This illustrates the attempt to integrate the multiple identities from the local, regional (Autonomous Community), central national state (Spain), and European to the broader global community. This is supported by the MEC (2006), as demonstrated by Article 17, which stated that education must focus on active citizenship promoting respect for human rights and a pluralist democratic society (Engel & Ortloff, 2009).

The Europeanization of Spanish curriculum becomes particularly significant in secondary education. Curricula at the secondary level include topics relating to the rights and duties of European citizens, EU institutions, contemporary European history (and Spain's role within the EU integration process), socio-cultural diversity, and economic issues related to the EU (Engel & Ortloff, 2009). Examining the Eurydice (2008) report for Spain, it is stated that:

> the fact that Spain is part of the European Union and the increasing number of immigrants in the Spanish society illustrate the importance of a knowledge of other languages and cultures within an environment of tolerance, respect, and solidarity. (p. 15)

These themes are present in the new educational legislation (MEC, 2006), in which the objectives of secondary education include themes of "tolerance, co-operation and solidarity between people and groups, dialogue, and common values of a pluralist society as preparation for democratic citizenship." Similar to primary curriculum, there is mention of the need to focus across local, regional (Autonomous Community), national state (Spain), European, and global levels.

REGIONALISM IN EUROPE

The overwhelming focus of the ever-expanding literature on the EU is a framing of the EU as an organization of nation states. This is not overwhelmingly surprising given its origins and history. In the context of the EU, Catalonia is considered a region, and is not recognized in the EU as "a nation...as Scotland or Wales are" (Guibernau, 2006, p. 220). As a region, Catalonia does not have access to EU policy-making institutions, and "is not a European electoral constituency" (Guibernau, 2006, p. 217). The Catalan language also has not gained official status in the EU. Yet, across the history of the development of the EU, regions have played a key role. As early as the 1957 Treaty of Rome, the Preamble stated that the original six members needed "to strengthen the unity of their economies and to ensure their harmonious development by reducing the differences existing between the various regions and the backwardness of the less favoured regions" (European Commission, 2000a, p. 5). In 1975, there were attempts to develop the poorest regions of Europe, which included the establishment of the European Regional Development Fund, which aimed to reallocate the budget contributions of Member State countries.

As the EU continuously developed through the 1990s, regions were provided even more developmental support. With the Maastricht Treaty of the early 1990s, cohesion became designated "as one of the main objectives of the Union, alongside economic and monetary union and the single market" (European Commission, 2000b, p. 5). The focus on cohesion stems in part from the need for economic development and the challenges posed by an ever-enlarging EU. Additionally, Jones and Keating (1995) argued that the 1980s enlargement to include southern states that possessed regional diversity, and the reorganization undertaken in a number of Member states resulted in a greater need to take the role of regions into account during the 1990s. Moreover, the authors showed that in the early 1990s "spending by the Community on regional policy had increased to around a quarter of its budget" (p. v). With the Maastricht Treaty, the EU's policy-making institutions changed, and regions developed particular decision-making capacities. As the EU focused on the economic development of the various regions in Europe, and cohesion became a significant policy objective, literature on the EU began to emphasize analyses of the role and the development of regions.

In the 1980s, scholarly work on the EU offered little analysis on the role of regions within the EU. However, as multilevel governance became a useful framework for political scientists and scholars in the social sciences in the 1990s, regions were provided increased attention. In this literature, there was a growing focus on the EU as an institution that has given rise to regions within their respective nation states (Closa & Heywood, 2004). Debates over the EU's regional policy have been rooted in diverse contexts, such as Catalonia and the Basque Country in Spain, the German Länder, and the Flemish in Belgium.

In each of these diverse contexts, advocates of greater regional representation in the EU have argued that above all, regions in the EU lead to greater citizen participation in EU decision-making and thus, greater democratization, which is a core aim of the new Europe. In the EU's development, regional policy has been emphasized as means for greater economic development and cooperation towards particular goals among all EU countries and citizens. In the European Commission (2000a) document, *Working for the Regions*, it was stated, "Europe's regional policy is above all a policy of solidarity....Regional policy is also a policy for people" (p. 3). The argument also follows that with an emphasis on the cultural diversity of EU regions, there is greater European economic integration.

It is helpful to distinguish two forms of regionalism, following the work of Keating (1995). Regionalism, Keating (1995) argued, can take many forms, two of which are top-down regionalism and bottom-up regionalism. Keating (1995) explained that top-down regionalism takes "the form of national regional policies," whereas bottom-up regionalism is "in the form of regional political and economic mobilization" (p. 2). The first, Keating (1995) discussed, related to many nation states in Europe and their policies towards regional development. Keating (1995) wrote,

> Economically, these [regional policies] were justified in terms of the need to tap under-utilized resources in peripheral and declining regions and increase national output. Politically, they served to enhance national solidarity and secure support from peripheral regions for the State regime or the party in power. (p. 2)

Many regions also possess long histories of independent cultural and linguistic traditions.

Keating (1995) discussed that at the same time as nation states in Europe emphasized regional development policies for economic and political purposes, many regions reasserted their "historical claims for regional and national distinctiveness" (p. 3). In the politics of European integration, the EU increasingly has become a forum, in which regions have the potential to gain greater autonomy from the central state. As Wright (2000) stated, "there is evidence that regions have found the umbrella of the EU as encouragement to bid for autonomy" (p. 179). The EU has also had an impact on the reshuffling of relationships and partnerships between regions, nation states, and the EU, in that new political alliances and networks are developing across regions, nations, and supranational levels. This is significant for education policy production and the intersection of different policy arenas, as well as policy priorities.

With the 1988 structural funds reform establishing a partnership principle between regions, nation states, and the EU, regions have increasingly gained representation in the context of the central state, as well as the EU. Giordano and Roller (2002) noted, "in recent years, regional entities as well as nationalist political parties have increasingly been able to further their demands within the international arena and to attract support for their causes both at home and abroad" (p. 101). This has raised questions regarding a Europe of the Regions (Applegate, 1999), or what MacLeod (1999) has referred to as Euro-supranationalism. Moreover, the institutional development of the Committee of the Regions (COR) and the principle of subsidiarity brings about an increase in regional authority and empowerment.

In the draft of the EU Constitution, regions are mentioned in Title 1, under relations between the EU and Member states. Article I-5.1 stated that the EU respects each of the Member states, "inclusive of regional and local self-government" (European Commission, 2004). The EU also has discussed regions in the Constitution in the context of safeguarding diversity. Article I-3.3 stated that the EU "shall respect rich cultural and linguistic diversity, and shall ensure that Europe's cultural heritage is safeguarded and enhanced" (European Commission, 2004). These views emphasized decentralization as a means of local and regional representation, means for greater EU integration, and the enhancement of economic development. After the failure of the Constitution, one of the key EU institutions focused on regional policy is the COR, which actively relies upon decentralization to execute EU policy-making and implementation.

The COR as an Institution

Leaders of the COR have argued that regional governance is especially needed after the failure of the EU Constitution in 2004, given the uneasiness of the citizens of France and the Netherlands about a EU suprastate. As the former President of the COR, Peter Straub (2005) stated, "referendums in France and the Netherlands have shown us that we have to really go to the citizen. We are closest to the citizens, the citizens trust us. This is why we can bring Europe closer to the citizen" (The Parliament, 2005, para. 7). Straub went on to note, "the best way forward, in my opinion, is decentralisation" (The Parliament, 2005, para. 19). The COR thought to be the means by which a common conception of Europe can be constructed. This has implications for notions of rescaling and the representation gained in specific regions that historically are not recognized by nation states. In recent years, with the new revised Lisbon Strategy, regions have been placed at the core of economic growth and the creation of jobs (The Parliament, 2009).

Officially developed by the Maastricht Treaty, the COR is an institution in Brussels that seeks to increase the participation of regions, cities, and local levels of governance. While established in 1994, its foundations can be traced back to the 1960 proposal by the European Parliamentary Assembly to set up a committee that could be consulted on matters of regional economies. As an institutional body, it provides a base for which local and regional government authorities and representatives are able to participate in EU policy-making. It also aims to create a place for regional and local identities and traditions within the larger space of European governance. As stated by the Local Government International Bureau (2005),

> The Maastricht Treaty resolved to create an ever closer union among the peoples of Europe. Through the COR, representatives of local and regional government are able to act as a link between local people and the EU institutions, thereby enabling decisions to be taken by representatives who are closest to the people. (para. 3)

The COR is an institution that seeks to increase the participation of regions, cities, and local levels of governance.

In negotiations prior to the signing of the Maastricht Treaty, Closa and Heywood (2004) argued that the COR was originally in response to the German Länder, as well as the Spanish autonomous communities (CCAA). They explained that primarily as a result of demands of the German Länder, the COR was developed in the early 1990s as a part of the Maastricht Treaty. The primary responsibility of the COR is to function as a consultative body, giving opinions to the Commission or the Council on new legislation and policy that have direct implications for regional and local policy. It is mandatory that the Council and the Commission consult the COR in policy-making in the following areas: education, training, culture, public health, fight against drugs, Trans-European Networks, social and economic cohesion, and structural funds. Depending on the specific policy area, the COR collaborates with the European Economic and Social Committee. There are other optional consultations that the COR may make. For example, the European Council, Commission, or Parliament may request a COR opinion when deemed appropriate, the COR may choose to prepare an opinion when the European Economic and Social Committee has been consulted and local and regional interests are at stake, or the COR may choose to prepare an opinion on its own initiative where considered appropriate.

Members of the COR include regional and local representatives, proposed by the Member states, those who are appointed formally by the Council, representatives of political groups and national delegations, and participants in thematic commissions. There are six thematic commissions represented in the COR (Territorial Cohesion Policy, Economic & Social Policy, Sustainable Development, Culture & Education, Constitutional Affairs, External Relations). It is noteworthy that the literature on the COR has pointed out that we must be cautious to not overemphasize the importance of the COR as a governance mechanism in the EU (Bale, 2005; Closa & Heywood, 2004; Wright, 2000). These authors have pointed out that the COR has had a supportive role in EU governance but little actual power as an institution. Nonetheless, it is helpful to focus on the aspects of the COR that may be more influential in ways that are not easily quantitatively measured and accounted.

To begin with, the COR provides a platform for regional and local authorities to voice their perspectives on EU policy-making and current legislative issues. The presence of local and regional actors in the EU helps localize regional interests. This is seen as the case for advocating that Catalan to be recognized as an official EU language (Closa & Heywood, 2004). Within Article 6 of Catalonia's 2006 Statute of Autonomy, under Section 3, it is stated that the Catalan government and the central state should take necessary steps to have Catalan be officially recognized in the EU.

On the issue of establishing Catalan as an official language of the EU, the regional offices of Catalonia and representatives of the COR have been very active. The EU encourages citizens to be able to speak two languages in addition to their first language, and the EU actively supports the teaching and learning of all EU languages. Article 126.2 of the Maastricht Treaty stated, "community action shall be aimed at developing the European dimension in education, particularly through the teaching and dissemination of the languages of the Member states" (European Commission, 1992). For example, the EU declared 2001 the Year of the Languages in recognition of the linguistic diversity within Europe (Jou & Meliá, 2002).

In recognition of linguistic diversity, Catalan is symbolically recognized as one of the languages of the EU. However, it is not recognized as an official institutional language of the EU, signifying that the EU does not have to provide funding for translation. According to a Generalitat of Catalonia (2002a) document, *Catalan, a European Language*, there are 11 million speakers of Catalan, which means that Catalan is spoken by more people than Finnish or Dannish, and compares with the number of speakers of Spanish, Greek, or Portuguese. Even languages, such as Maltese, which has about 400,000 speakers, are official EU languages. In recent years, following extensive pressure from the Catalan government both in Madrid and Brussels, the Spanish government has now been allowed to pay for its own Catalan translators. The Spanish government currently pays for a small cadre of Catalan translators.

The EU also looks at the COR as a means of improving upon governance and a vehicle for involving regional and local representatives. Not only does it provide a forum for local and regional voices to be expressed in Brussels, which may not be spoken for within the context of the nation state, but the COR also allows Europe a mechanism for becoming closer to its citizens and furthering the process of European integration. As a form of European governance, the COR provides regions with increased access and representation in the processes of policy production, which may not be spoken for in the context of EU institutional arrangements. The COR is also a vehicle for implementing Commission policies.

While the European Commission adopts a top-down mechanism of policy-making, there was a need for an institutional body to focus on policy implementation. In Taylor et al.'s work (1997), the authors stressed the idea of policy as a set of processes involving production, negotiation, and implementation. In other words, implementation is vital to the development of policy and the COR is viewed as a crucial part of the policy process in terms of its role in policy implementation.

As an example, the intentions of policy in its construction do not always transfer in its implementation, given the complex negotiations and conflicting ideologies present. In the context of the EU, the COR is seen as a body of governance acting as a middle-person of sorts, providing regional and local input in on the development of EU legislation and policy, as well as in turn advocating the practice of EU policies in local and regional contexts. As the President of the COR, Peter Straub (2005) stated, "they [the EU] need the regional level, they need the regions, the cities to put political intentions into practice" (The Parliament, 2005). Therefore, not only does the COR function as a forum for local and supranational representation, but it also is the means of policy implementation.

The COR as a Mechanism of Governance

In addition, the COR is a central strategic mechanism in the broader construction project of a cohesive Europe (Shore, 2000). Popkewitz (2000) has argued that

> the governing patterns embodied in the new constructions of EU's Europe entail new reconfigurations in the nexus of nationality-sovereignty-citizenship that cannot be taken for granted in studies of 'European identity' but need to be explored through the new principles of governing produced. (p. 6)

In this way, the COR functions as a mechanism for the EU to get closer to its citizens and further the process of European integration. Calhoun (2004) reasoned that Europe, if seeking to reach past its establishment as purely a place, must forge and institutionalize a distinctive, and common Euro-identity, woven with a shared future vision among its citizens underlie the construction and development of distinct political and social institutions.

Following the discussion of the multiple forms of decentralization, the EU has increasingly supported decentralization as a means of enhancing system efficiency. Balcells (1996) argued, "decentralization was forced on highly centralist states by reason of the inefficiency of public administration when faced with wider responsibilities. The Brussels administration cannot but follow the same road" (p. 200). Along with the argument in support of a more administrative form of decentralization as means of greater efficiency, the EU also has developed particular mechanisms of governance to further the project of European integration. In this way, the COR operates as a mode of governance, operating as close to the citizen as possible.

The COR, given that it relies upon decentralization to share knowledge about and implement EU policies, can be analyzed as a central strategic mechanism in the broader construction project of a cohesive Europe. Shore (2000) examined these modes of EU governance as the exercising of "political technologies," referring to the ways in which knowledge shapes how individual citizens naturally conduct themselves in a manner conducive to the new norms set by the EU. The role of the COR has "deep ramifications for the way Europe is constructed and reflected in the mind's eye of the public" (Shore, 2000, p. 31). Within European integration is the underlying project of building a European citizenry, in which the COR is a core institution. The "forces through which knowledge of EU is embodied and communicated as a socio-cultural phenomenon...all helping to engender awareness and promote acceptance of European idea," are reflected in the institutions, such as the COR, which actively promotes the construction of a European consciousness by being located at the local and regional levels (Shore, 2000, p. 26). The mechanisms by which the EU attempts to "govern from a distance" can be identified concretely by new modes of governance, such as in the case of decentralization.

In the EU's quest for continued integration, it approached the tension between a Europe of the Nations versus a Europe of the Regions. As regions increasingly push for cultural and linguistic recognition and enhanced jurisdiction to participate in EU affairs, questions arise as to how well equipped the EU is to handle these demands. Yet, in order for the European integration project to be successful, the EU actively seeks mechanisms to get as close to the citizen as possible. In this way, the EU draws on regional and local authorities for its own purposes, in much of the same way that regions like Catalonia look towards the EU. Consequently, the relations between regions and nation states have become reconfigured by the EU, and are no longer neatly funneled into center-periphery and Europe-nation state frameworks. The following section looks at the case of Catalonia, Spain, and the EU more specifically.

COOPERATION, CONTESTATION, AND MEDIATION

It is part of Spain, yet it also looks outward.
(Giddens, 1999)

The EU has historically existed as a common model of modernization for both the Spanish state and Catalonia. Giordano and Roller (2002) wrote, "'Europe provided a unifying objective" (p. 104). This is shown in the context of education. For example, as the EU has pressed forward with the Bologna Process, a move to harmonize the higher education systems of EU countries, the reaction from Catalonia and more broadly, from Spain, is in opposition. One former policy-maker from the Ministry of Education in Madrid argued, "Spaniards are opposed to Bologna, all of the rest of Europe supports it, it is an extraordinary thing. But the Spaniards remain...against Bologna" (personal communication). The EU's educational programs, such as Bologna have been interpreted in such a way that aligns European integration with a particular neoliberal interpretation of globalization. In Spain, there is a very strong anti-globalization movement. This movement has incorporated interpretations of EU educational programs and policy agendas into what is believed to be a global agenda to privatize education.

Cooperation

During one of my visits to the Autonomous University of Barcelona during the summer of 2005, as typical throughout Spain and Catalonia, there was politically oriented graffiti that covered walls and signs on campus. I visited the campus during several protests held during the process of implementing reforms of the Bologna Treaty. In the middle of the university campus, was a message in Castilian Spanish painted across the concrete steps: "No Bologna, We are not a Market. Universities are not Markets." The former policy-maker of the Ministry of Education described this sentiment among Catalan students and community members. He stated, "it is very funny actually because the Catalan nationalists prefer to side with Spaniards that are opposed to Bologna. They talk about privatization" (personal communication). He then went on to interpret the movement of opposition to the EU's educational agenda as a unifying issue for all citizens of Spain, so much so that the Catalan movement for greater autonomy and self-government is overshadowed in the process.

The EU also has been a factor of intergovernmental support between the CCAA. In interviews with two policy-makers in Barcelona, they described responsibilities of regional offices in Brussels to include the translation of documents and information. The offices then communicate this information to their respective regional government departments in promotion of regional interests. These regions also support the COR and regularly participate in regional meetings in Brussels. One significant issue that emerged during interviews with regional policy-makers involved the change in the intergovernmental relationship between the CCAA in the context of the EU. One participant described the relations between CCAA to be "non-existent" in the context of Spain, but "very cooperative" within Brussels (personal communication). The CCAA often cooperate and communicate about projects and discussions in Brussels that affect regional interests, while in Spain, they often do not or are unable to cooperate.

Contestation

However, the EU has also served as a major point of conflict between the central Spanish state and the CCAA, particularly Catalonia and the Basque Country. The ideal of the EU as a new domain in which historical regional demands can resurface has been promoted in Catalonia, even if this ideal of the EU has remained vague. Keating (1995) argued that in Catalonia, "Europe is evoked more vaguely, as providing an arena in which the regional personality can be projected and as an alternative frame of reference to the State" (p. 8). The role that the EU plays in relations between Spain and Catalonia remains ambiguous. In the post-Franco era, while Catalonia has increased powers of governance and shared responsibilities with the central government, as stated in the previous chapter, the Spanish Constitution remains ambiguous regarding the participation of the CCAA in international or EU affairs (Closa & Heywood, 2004). Drawing on the example of constitutional ambiguity in Spain and the EU, there have been many conflicts over the role of the CCAA in foreign policy. One example involves the establishment of CCAA offices in Brussels.

In 1986, with Spain's accession into the EC, the Basque Country and Catalonia immediately established regional offices in Brussels. The central Spanish state questioned the legality of regional representation in Brussels, and argued that it undermined Spanish national unity in foreign matters (Closa & Heywood, 2004). The case was brought to the Constitutional Tribunal, which ruled in 1995 that CCAA could in fact participate in foreign affairs under the condition that they not act against Spain's foreign policy (Closa & Heywood, 2004). Since 1995, all of the Spanish CCAA have had regional offices in Brussels. Even with the regional offices in the EU, the central state has not allowed Catalonia and the other CCAA to freely participate in international affairs. For example, any visit that the Catalan president makes abroad has to be communicated with the central state (personal communication).

Generally, it is considered that foreign policy is the jurisdiction of the Spanish central state. One central government official explained

> the [CCAA] can have their own external relations...it's like defense. Defense is the jurisdiction of the central state, but each CCAA can have their own autonomous police, like [Catalonia's] Mosso d'Esquadra, but they have to work in coordination with the state police and security forces. With foreign policy, Catalonia has to work in line with the central state. (personal communication)

Foreign policy has been a source of conflict for the central state and Catalonia. A participant reflected: "the central state is not very keen on the international role of the [CCAA] but it has to accept it because the Constitutional Tribunal has accepted [regional] offices in Brussels" (personal communication). Still, the central policy maker in Madrid went on to state that any of the CCAA "can open offices around the world, teach their regional languages to whomever all they want, but they can still not bypass the competencies of the state" (personal communication). In this way, the central Spanish state's foreign policy is utilized to exercise a significant amount of authority over Catalonia and the other CCAA.

With these examples, the debate continues over the extent to which regions can even participate in the EU. Roller (2004) wrote that "greater representation and participation in the EU's institutions have become an increasingly salient issue in Catalonia, particularly in light of the Spanish government's more marked refusal to agree to anything other than indirect participation" (p. 82). During an interview with an educational official in Barcelona, a government official discussed the debates regarding central Spanish state educational offices in Brussels and whether or not they should be decentralized to Catalonia and the other CCAA.

This is a central issue, the participant explained, because some of the educational policies that are being developed at the Catalan level for the interests of Catalonia depend directly on Brussels, and do not depend on the central state. However, while there is a major push to decentralize the control of European offices in Brussels to regional levels of the CCAA, the authority to decentralize still remains in the hands of the central state. This control, one participant stated, "is something that they [the central government] will never give us" (personal communication). It was also the general view among participants that until Catalonia has its own foreign policy and can act independently in the context of the EU, it will remain a nation seeking statehood.

Mediation

Additionally, the EU has been looked at as a mediating force to help solve conflicts evoked in a decentralized model of the Spanish state. In the case of the CCAA of Spain, the EU is emphasized as an institution, which can serve to solve conflicts between CCAA and the central state. Pereyra's (2002) study of decentralization and centralization in Spain looked specifically at two CCAA: Andalusia and the Canary Islands. These two regions have been ranked as two of the poorest CCAA in Spain and least developed regions in the EU. The study examines the tensions that have arisen in the transition of the Spanish state.

Pereyra (2002) reported that all participants viewed the central government as possessing a lack of sufficient knowledge and capacity for the management of the decentralized education system, especially as some of the CCAA, such as Catalonia, continue to pursue policies to gain increased autonomy. With regards to the EU, Pereyra (2002) wrote that participants in the study "make references to alternative power bases beyond the central state-for example the [EU]" (p. 672). The participants also believed that the EU is not advocating strongly enough for "consensus among countries in educational matters" (Pereyra, 2002, p. 672). The reactions from system actors from Andalusia and the Canary Islands suggest that the EU is viewed as a mediating force for internal state affairs, as well as the intergovernmental conflicts arising among the CCAA. In this sense, the EU has been interpreted as an institution above the state that is able to help establish national unity in the face of what is perceived to be fragmentation brought on by a decentralized structure.

Across the varied reflections on the project for a new Europe and its impact both in Spain and Catalonia, it seems that in recent years, the EU has become a key education policy actor, with a clear educational agenda that is actively being reflected in national education systems, such as Spain. In the EU, a particular framework for education has been developed, referred to in this chapter as a European education policy space. This has included the development of educational programs according to the EU's political, economic, and social vision. While system actors interviewed often regarded the EU's efforts as having little to no effect on education policy in Spain and Catalonia, the development of a European education policy space has involved the development of new performance standards, indicators, and benchmarks.

These mechanisms of "soft law" have allowed the EU to construct what is currently a very powerful space for areas of education policy reform that align with EU aims and goals (Trubek & Trubek, 2005). One of these instruments is the OMC, which has aligned policy discourses with the interests of the EU and other Member states. The OMC has also sparked comparisons of policies and practices between Member State countries. The development of a European education policy space also has reconfigured educational governance and reshuffled the relationships between regions, nation states, and the EU. As the EU has reconfigured educational governance, it drastically has rearranged and realigned policy production across regions and nation states. The chapter examined this through the EU's emphasis on a particular form of decentralization and the institutional role of the COR. I argue that these realignments of governance actively disrupt dominant frameworks of educational governance policy production.

Scholars often presume the policy stronghold of the nation state over its educational system. As shown in this chapter, global processes have disrupted these analyses and focused on the ways in which political and economic organizations, such as the EU, are impacting educational systems. While states are becoming increasingly integrated with the EU, regions are forced to play significant roles. This occurs at the same time as the EU has become an arena for regional nationalists to assert their own demands. In the following chapter, I work to tie in the analyses of this chapter and chapter 4. In doing so, I examine this complex, dynamic overlap of multiple political spaces through the notion of rescaling.

RESCALING AND THE POLITICS OF DECENTRALIZATION

Policy is both text and action, words and deeds, it is what is enacted as well as what is intended. Policies are always incomplete in so far as they relate to or map on to 'wild profusion' of local practice.
(Ball, 1994, p. 10)

Chapter 3 focused on the politics of the shifting relationship between Catalonia and the central Spanish state, and the impact of these changes on education policy formation. This includes a number of developments in the form of decentralization. Chapter 4 traced the ways in which education policy has been produced during the democratic transition and the contemporary post-Franco era. In the chapter, I highlighted key policy pressures within the state that appeared to be shaping the formation of education policy, and debates about policies such as the revised Statute of Autonomy and the National Pact for Education.

The previous chapter examined shifts in education policy production in relation to pressures that emanate from EU priorities and broader global processes. Chapter 5 traced a number of analyses revolving around the appearance of states and their policy agendas as increasingly becoming aligned to what is perceived to be global economic imperatives. In the context of the argument that IOs and supranational organizations have become increasingly powerful in reshaping educational discourses in national systems, Chapter 5 highlighted the EU specifically, and provided a historical backdrop to the EU's political, economic, social, and cultural aims that have developed into a European education policy space. This included new policy developments, including international performance standards and benchmarks. In chapter 5, I also discussed the EU's promotion of decentralization as a mechanism to press for its aims of greater integration and economic efficiency.

In this chapter, I aim to tie in these analyses presented in the two previous chapters. This is purposefully carried out under the premise that in order to understand the changing dynamics of education policy formation processes in relation to decentralization in the particular context of the Catalonia, it has become increasingly important to understand processes of nation state rescaling. First, the notion of rescaling is discussed, which involves a number of crosscurrents, which are contingent, uneven, historically specific, and are driven by political struggles negotiated by particular agents. Therefore, the first part of this chapter explores the notion of rescaling and some of the ways in which it has been thought about in relation to contemporary debates of globalization. I argue that rescaling cannot be understood without first considering the particular actors that are involved in negotiating and producing scale. To illustrate these shifts, I explore the ways in which rescaling is emerging through discourses of decentralization that are being interpreted, negotiated, and formulated across multiple scales. In the process of mapping out the interpretations made by educational actors across a dynamic and complex series of multiscalar interactions, rescaling becomes an important concept to understand the reconfiguration of state space and new modes of governance produced.

RESCALING THE STATE

In contemporary debates of globalization, the notion of scale has become increasingly significant. First in geography and more currently by scholars in a range of disciplines, "scale" has been used to examine political, economic, social, and cultural relations that cut across a complex set of horizontal and vertical spatial configurations (Brenner, 2001, 2004; Smith, 2003). As pointed out by Smith (2003), "geographical scale is traditionally treated as a neutral metric of physical space" (p. 228). However, scholars now understand that "geographical scales of human activity are not neutral 'givens', not fixed universals of social experience, nor are they an arbitrary methodological or conceptual choice" (Smith, 2003, p. 228). Smith (2003) went on to state that "far from neutral and fixed...geographical scales are the product of economic, political and social activities and relationships" and "different kinds of society produce different kinds of geographical scale for containing and enabling particular forms of social interaction" (p. 228). As scale is socially and politically constructed, literature has discussed rescaling as a process in order to examine the ways in which political, territorial, and economic configurations are actively broken down and remade.

Rescaling is a concept that is used to encompass trends that involve the layering of governance across various political spaces that are not automatically situated within state functions. Rather than treating developments of globalization and Europeanization as end products or static outcomes, rescaling allows for a perspective on the process of spatial reconfiguration (Brenner, 2004). Smith (2003) argued that

> *production of scale*, therefore, is a highly charged and political process as is the continual reproduction of scale at established levels (e.g., defence of national boundaries, community tax base, regional identity). Even more politically charged is the reproduction of scale at different levels—the restructuring of scale, the establishment of new 'scale fixes' for new concatenations of political, economic and cultural interchange. (p. 229; author's italics)

The production of scale, however, is not the making and remaking of a hierarchical order of space that already is existent, in which space is considered static and depoliticized (Massey, 2005). Notions of scale should not be treated as insular entities or clearly demarcated hierarchies. Brenner (2001) wrote, "scale...cannot be construed adequately as a system of territorial containers defined by absolute geographic size (a 'Russian dolls' model of scales)," in which the local fits neatly within the regional, regional within the national, national within the supranational, etc. (p. 605-606). Rather, the process of rescaling is "fluid and dynamic" (Marston & Smith, 2001, p. 616). This brings to light the formulation and shifts of relations among and across scales.

In Brenner's (2004) work, he has presented a number of methodological challenges related to scale. I want to briefly highlight two of them as they relate to the focus of this book. The first challenge is "conceptualizing scale as a *process* (for instance, of localization, regionalization, nationalization, or globalization) rather than as a permanently fixed, pregiven thing" and the second challenge is, "conceptualizing the intrinsic *relationality* of all geographical scales and their embeddedness within broader interscalar hierarchies" (Brenner, 2004, p. 8). In this book, notions of scale and rescaling have been discussed as dynamic and widely debated concepts utilized to engage processes of education policy formation within a reconfigured state. These notions have been useful for an examination of new modes of governance produced in education, especially in relation to the politics of shifting articulations of decentralization.

These new shifts of governance appear to be the state's strategic response to its consistent negotiation of multiple pressures. Consequently, education policy production processes are becoming increasingly complex, given the myriad of pressures emanating from global, supranational, national, regional, and local scales. As Brenner, Jessop, Jones, and MacLeod (2003) stated

the scalar organization of state space—from the global level of the inter-state system and the national level of state territoriality to subnational tiers of governance such as regional, local, and neighorhood-level institutions—is never fixed forever. Instead, in conjunction with broader socio-economic pressures, constraints, and transformations, it is liable to recurrent redesign, restructuring, and reorientation. (p. 5)

This raises critical questions about the nature of education policy production, not only in light of our understanding of the state's role in developing policy, but also of policy production from within the overlap of political scales.

Over the past 30 years, the Spanish state has undergone a dramatic reinvention as a result of democratization and the construction of the State of Autonomies, decentralization and the recognition of 17 CCAA, Europeanization and Spain's on going participation in the construction of the new Europe, and broader global pressures. As Brenner (2004) aptly wrote, rescaling processes take place in "the wake of intense sociopolitical struggles" (p. 11). The intersection of these various pressures has situated the production of education policy in a multilateral crossfire of diverse and often contrasting aims of education. As Giordano and Roller (2002) aptly noted, "what is emerging within Europe is a complex political order in which European politics is becoming more regionalized; regional politics is increasingly Europeanized; and national politics is both Europeanized and regionalized" (p. 100). Consequently, the formation of a multiscalar policy stage is becoming increasingly crowded with various system actors, including IOs, supranational organizations like the EU, national ministries, regional departments of education, national and regional unions for parents, teachers, and students, city councils, administrators, and local educational agencies, among others.

Additionally, in what is conceived as the 1980s neoliberal state "roll-back" (Tickell & Peck, 2003), local and regional governments were provided with increased responsibilities over the public sector. This occurred at the same time as global pressures ignited the need for national economies to draw upon local and regional strengths to meet the needs of a changing economy (Jeffery, 2002; Tickell & Peck, 2003). Brenner (2004) argued

> In contrast to the highly centralized, hierarchical, and vertically integrated national administrative frameworks that prevailed during the Fordist-Keynesian period, the post-1980s wave of decentralization established new subnational layers of state institutional organization and regulatory activity through which major local and regional political-economic actors—and, in some cases, local and regional populations—could more directly influence subnational policy outcomes. (p. 20)

In the EU specifically, this resulted in a complex set of relations and interactions across local, regional, national, supranational, and global terrains. As a result of these developments, regional governance has become increasingly significant within the EU. As Jeffery (2002) noted, "at such critical moments as these, negotiating agendas [we]re fluid and windows of opportunity for new and often unanticipated initiatives c[ould] emerge" (p. 328). The Committee of the Regions (COR), and a Catalan presence in Brussels is the result of this particular spatial and temporal shifts.

As discussed in the previous chapter, it is worth nothing that the COR has a "particular historical context...[in] the more fluid dynamics of the early 1990s 'multi-level governance'" (Jeffery, 2002, p. 327). In addition, in the contemporary era of globalization, regional and local level governance has been viewed as fundamental for increased economic growth and the creation of a leaner central government, as influenced by neoliberal perspectives. In Europe, there also have been pressures from the ground up, in particular with the German Länder's proposal of regional representation at the EU level. The Länder strategically teamed up with other regional authorities, such as the Flemish in Belgium and the Catalans in Spain, to help push the agenda for a regional representative body. Thus, as Jeffrey (2002) argued the context in which the COR emerged was a very "odd alliance of 'top-down' *and* 'bottom-up', technocratic *and* representative agendas" (p. 331).

I want to argue that it is within this complex overlap of contrasting interests, aims, imperatives, and pressures, rather than state functions alone, that education policy pertaining to governance are produced, negotiated, implemented, and reformed. Rescaling is an important concept that allows for an understanding of these complex intersections and multiple pressures, and the ways in which they are actively being interpreted and negotiated in the production of education policy. However, in conceptualizing rescaling in education policy production, actors doing the interpreting and negotiating must be brought to the forefront of analysis.

The relationship between these multiple actors and the production of education policy has been addressed thus far in this book. Even as rescaling and the production of scale has been discussed in relation to "intense sociopolitical struggles," often times, this literature is absent of the actors who are taking account and negotiating what is happening at multiple scales in relation to policy formation (Brenner, 2004, p. 11). This book has aimed to bring actors' negotiations to the forefront of policies related to educational governance, specifically decentralization in Spain. Through the perspectives, experiences, and reflections of actors shaping the interactions taking place across multiple spaces, rescaling becomes conceptualized as a process that is highly complex, widely debated, and politically and historically contingent.

Across the two previous chapters, chapters 4 and 5, this book has attempted to trace the policies produced in relation to educational decentralization. This has included the political and economic shifts in the Spanish state, and the territorial reconfiguration as a result of democratization, decentralization, Europeanization with Spain's membership in the EU, and broader global processes. The study of these processes stands against the literature on education policy production, which typically has relied upon linear, hierarchical analyses from the global to the local, and been conceptualized using models such as top-town, bottom-up, margin-center, and center-periphery. It also counters the pervasive state-centrism and methodological nationalism embedded in the literature in the social sciences and education.

Thus far, the analysis has been divided between pressures from below in chapter 5 and above in chapter 5, and their impact on education policy production from a spatial and scalar perspective. Therefore, even in the context of this project, the division of pressures conceptualized as either from above or from below the state seems to suggest the "opposition between the 'domestic' and the 'foreign'" (Brenner, Jessop, Jones & MacLeod, 2003, p. 2). While these concepts have been helpful thus far in the analytical framing and organizing of this book, the following section aims to bring to light the process of rescaling and the interactions being formed across local, regional, national, supranational, and global scales with respect to education policy production concerning decentralization.

REARTICULATING DECENTRALIZATION

Hierarchies, such as the global to the local and local to the global offer a false sense of simplicity among the multiple and complex interactions taking place within and across numerous scales. The following illustration of the politics of decentralization aims to move away from the privileging of one scale—the national, which is often the case in studies of globalization and education policy formation—and problematize the standard ways that educational decentralization has been through about and conceptualized. Across local, regional, national, supranational, and global scales, the politics of decentralization are shifting, becoming "rearticulated" consistently in relation to shifting scales, to such an extent that it is difficult to present any clear cut view of what the local, regional, national, supranational, and global represents (Daryl Slack, 2006). In what follows, I draw on empirical evidence generated from interviews and documents in an attempt to play out debates about decentralization as a result of a range of multiscalar, interactional pressures. Across these scales, the agency of human actors is foregrounded to illustrate the different ways that actors are interpreting and encountering these multiple pressures differently.

Debates over educational decentralization appear to be informed largely by the interactions taking place across local, regional, national, and supranational scales, as well as policy actors' engagement with ideas and ideologies circulating around the global space. In the context of this study, interviews conducted with actors in Barcelona and Madrid, and documents collected in Barcelona, Madrid, and Brussels, suggest the interconnections taking place across scales. These multiple interconnections represent a disruption of the traditional ways of conceptualizing power relations between the center and periphery.

Moreover, by examining the shifts in decentralization across local, regional, national, supranational, and global scales, there is an extension of the current literature on decentralization in Spain, which limits analysis to relations between the central Spanish state and regions, such as Catalonia. Lastly, multiscalar interactions taking place suggest that the politics of decentralization are shifting in such a way that it is no longer possible to clearly delineate divisions between scales. The following sub-sections offer different interpretations of education policy involving decentralization from policy actors at local, regional, national and supranational scales. In the discussion that follows, I outline multiple interpretations of Europe and different interpretations of pressures emerging from a European education policy space.

Local Policy Actors

Reflections of local actors on educational decentralization disrupt the binary frameworks, such as center-periphery, bottom-up, and top-down, so often used in the attempt to capture the politics of decentralization. In interviews with local policy actors in Barcelona, it appears that regional, national, EU, and global pressures are at the forefront of policy negotiations. In debates over educational decentralization in Barcelona, there has been a political move to deepen decentralization to local municipal and administrative bodies. This is evident in the National Pact for Education (2006) document and its predecessor in 2005, which established a series of educational issues to be debated for inclusion in the finalized 2006 National Pact. One of the central issues presented in both the 2005 and 2006 documents is greater autonomy for educational centers as means of increasing the quality of education in Catalonia.

During the Francoist era, there was little public financial support provided by the central state to local schools. As discussed in earlier chapters, the first half of authoritarian Francoist dictatorship was marked by the creation of a highly centralized and isolationist state, while the latter half involved a major overhaul of the Spanish economy to embrace market liberalization. Across both of these periods, regional languages and cultural traditions were condemned and banned in schools across Spain, to be replaced by Castilian Spanish as the only language of instruction to be used in schools throughout Spain. Catalan, the language of Catalonia, also was banned on the street, in print, in schools, in politics, and in communication.

In the Francoist regime's preoccupation with stability, the educational system in Spain was highly centralized in the promotion of nationalist rhetoric and Catholic values. During the forty year dictatorship, the purpose of public education was to construct a Spanish citizenry around nationalism, a centralized military state, and Catholicism. Given that the Spanish state was unable and unwilling to financially support the Spanish education system, the Catholic Church was especially important, as it was charged with the organization, regulation, and funding of Spanish public schools. While used to promote the central values of the Francoist state, the Spanish public education system became marked by the sheer absence of the state. Moreover, the long absence of the state in education became a primary issue during Spain's transition to democracy after Franco's death in 1975. One education policy-maker in Barcelona stated

> When the dictatorship was over and we shifted into a democracy, in this process, one of the things that we detected was what little investment the state had made in Catalonia's educational system...and the immense quantity of private schools that were run by co-ops of parents and teachers. (personal communication)

Independent, private educational centers were developed during the Francoist era as a way in which to continue to offer quality education in Barcelona. Local actors also reflected upon not only the historical absence of the central Spanish state but also the deficiency of the regional Catalan government, placing more pressure on local governments and infrastructure.

During the Francoist and post-Franco era, local educational leaders argued that similar to the central state, the regional government in Catalonia was unable or unwilling to provide for local educational centers. However, in spite of the lack of financial support and necessary infrastructure, local actors reflected on the ways in which the Spanish central government, with support of the regional government in Catalonia, developed educational laws that called for free and compulsory education for all Spanish primary and secondary age citizens.

Consequently, construction of the necessary infrastructure to support the increasing demand of educational enrollment was left up to local level governments. One educational leader in Barcelona explained, "the most important educational initiatives were made by the city councils to create more schools and develop more educational space for students" (personal communication). This educational leader went on to state,

> what the state was not doing during the Francoist era, or what the Generalitat also was not doing either because it did not have any money or it just was not a priority, education was left to be covered by the power of the city councils. (personal communication)

These interpretations of local system actors disrupt the traditional ways that decentralization has been examined as the neat organization of power relations between the center and periphery. In the case of Spain especially, decentralization has been limited to the study of relations between the central state and regions, such as Catalonia.

In the current policy negotiations and debates taking place in Catalonia, however, the politics of decentralization seem to be shifting across and within multiple scales. Actors at the local level, for example, reflected on the struggle for greater autonomy over education policy from the central state and the regional Catalan government, often relying on what they believe to be a local historically embedded consciousness about quality education. Local actors argued that both the regional and national levels were unable and/or unwilling to provide local educational systems with the necessary financial support and the legislative competencies to produce policies that would lead to a better quality education. One local educational leader in Barcelona argued

the city councils' [educational] responsibilities were increased given the absence of the state, not because they were more or less prepared than the rest of Spain. Rather, it was because of the necessity that there was to give concrete answers to existing problems. (personal communication)

With the 2006 National Pact for Education in Catalonia, local government actors were pressing for increased educational autonomy from both regional and national governments. One leader in Barcelona stated, "it is very sensible that the city councils in Barcelona are asking for greater autonomy, not to have more power, but rather because the closer to the problem the government can get, the better the problems can be resolved" (personal communication). In current policy negotiations, local educational leaders appeared to interpret policies of decentraization emanating from regional and national levels as a unilateral form of decentralization.

Participants at the local level also discussed the unfinished process of democratization and decentralization, which they argued would culminate when local educational centers have the competencies to make policy decisions over curriculum, administration, and management. This perspective is similar to the views of regional actors in Catalonia, who reflected on their engagement with the local pressures to decentralize, predominantly given the importance of Barcelona as the capital city and economic, political, and cultural powerhouse of Catalonia. Similar to local actors, with the National Pact for Education in Catalonia signed in 2006, regional educational actors predominantly discussed the topic of decentralizing power to the local administrative levels as a form of increasing democratization and the quality of education. Regional actors' interpretations reveal the importance of locality in order to recover an ownership of the political history of Barcelona and Catalonia, and its linguistic and cultural heritage. Decentralization, in this way, is a political form of reengaging with Catalonia and Barcelona's political, cultural, and linguistic history independent of that of the central Spanish state.

Regional Policy Actors

In relation to the multiple scales of governance, actors at the regional level appears to be interpreting the politics of decentralization as a way to push forward with an overarching agenda of regional identity politics. In a number of interviews with educational leaders and authorities in Catalonia, participants stated that Catalonia was a leader in driving the process of decentralization: "Catalonia is absolutely a pioneer in the politics of decentralization" (personal communication). In the process of democratization, Catalonia has been central in pressing for a more political form of decentralization.

The idea of political decentralization first emerged in the immediate aftermath of the death of Franco, and the emergence of a new democratic state in Spain. Roller (2004) has referred to this as the "first phase" of decentralization (p. 94). A politically motivated form of decentralization typically is utilized as an attempt to meet local and regional demands, and to inspire local and regional empowerment. In Spain, political decentralization marks the reform of the Spanish state during the transition period. As discussed in chapter 4, the first of the CCAA of Spain to receive policy-making powers were Catalonia and the Basque Country, both classified as historical nations in the 1978 Constitution. These two CCAA did not have to formally apply in order to receive the powers allotted under the new decentralized organization (Heywood, 1995). Instead, powers were decentralized to Catalonia and the Basque Country in 1979 and 1980, immediately following the adoption of the Spanish Constitution. This was based on the status held by Catalonia and the Basque Country during the Second Republic in the 1930s.

In the process of constructing and unrolling the new democratic Spanish state, Catalonia and the Basque Country continued to press for greater decision-making authorities. Guibernau (2006) wrote that to proceed with this reform, "the political forces in Spain considered it necessary to grant some kind of political recognition of Catalan specificity, which was defended by a powerful social movement of a democratic and nationalist nature" (p. 217). However, during the period immediately following the construction of the Spanish State of Autonomies, reactions to the new Spanish decentralized state were marked by "disenchantment" (Guibernau, 2006, p. 217). In this historical period, Guibernau (2006) stated, "many Catalans were progressively disappointed by insufficient autonomous funding and a slow and costly process of transferring powers from the central government to the autonomous institutions" (p. 217). The disappointment was fueled by the promotion of decentralization as political means of greater local citizen empowerment in the process of democratization.

The ways in which regional actors in Catalonia appeared to interpret the national level in terms of decentralization policies suggests a historically rooted lack of trust and confidence in the central Spanish state. One regional educational government official in Catalonia explained that the resistance from Catalonia to central state policies is more extensive than other CCAA.

> There are autonomies that are happy when the state is doing something and telling them what to do…also with Europe, now Catalonia has some money

coming from Madrid and in Catalonia, the public says 'why is Madrid giving us money? These are our competencies. They should not be doing this,' and other autonomies are saying 'fine, we are receiving money from Madrid'.... There is a certain tendency that is really a cultural issue at the end of the day...a very deeply-rooted cultural issue. (personal communication)

In chapter 4, the reflections of system actors appeared to collectively demonstrate an interpretation of national policies of decentralization being a way for the central Spanish government to control education without appearing to control education. Decentralization and regional or local voice emphasized as significant; yet, in reality, the significant policy decisions and educational legislation is developed by the central state. This is what Karlsen (2000) has referred to as decentralized centralism.

One education policy-maker stated, "the process of decentralization has been very limited. The best indicator of this is if we had really created a decentralized country, we would not have the LOE, we would have the LOE for each autonomous community" (personal communication). Furthermore, as an administrative form of decentralization, the state controls the production of policies, "but it bears no responsibilities for their implementation" (personal communication). Within policies of decentralization, as noted previously, Catalonia has been central in advocating for a more political form of decentralization.

Even as the central Spanish government presented LOAPA in the early 1980s in an attempt to slow the process of decentralization, including in Catalonia and the Basque Country, the subsequent ruling by the Constitutional Tribunal showed that Catalonia and the Basque Country were powerful and could not be ignored by the central state over issues pertaining to their autonomous rights. In education, a more political form of decentralization also was advocated, as evidenced by the example of Catalonia's refusal to implement the humanities curriculum policy developed by the central Spanish government in 1997. These tensions in the ways that the regional level interprets what is happening at the national level are deeply historical and embedded in the way that Catalonia constructs itself within the long history of military, political, and cultural landscape in Spain.

National Policy Actors

Reflections on educational decentralization shifted in discussions with national actors, who emphasized the challenge that democratization and Europeanization posed, particularly in the necessity to spark economic growth and ensure social cohesion during a period of global economic crisis. These challenges that the Spanish central government faced during the transition created an alternative conception of the role of decentralization, one that combines the goals of political and administrative decentralization. For example, national policy-makers and political actors viewed decentralization as a means of consolidating democratization, responding to the demands of minority nationalist movements, and freeing up resources by a downsizing of central bureaucratic costs.

Similar to the reflections of regional actors, at the national level, system actors revealed that the politics of decentralization are rooted in a historical set of complex processes. One high level government official in the MEC, as it was previously known, in Madrid stated "we have historically had a problem with two autonomous communities: Catalonia and Euskadi [Basque Country], which is a problem whose origin lies in historical processes" (personal communication). In discussing the impact of historical processes on current debates over decentralization, this government official went on to state that both the Constitution and the State of Autonomies are efforts in recognizing the reality of "national pluralism in Spain" (personal communication). The ways in which national actors perceived of issues in Catalonia were also rooted in historical processes of cultural and political identity formation.

Another educational authority in the MEC in Madrid stated, "Catalonia has publicly acknowledged its historical, political, and cultural identity...although in truth, the last year of the revision of the Statute [of Autonomy in Catalonia] has been very conflictive" (personal communication). During the 2006 process of revising and approving the new Statute of Autonomy in Catalonia, as discussed in chapter 4, autonomy and the concept of a Catalan nation were equated with separatism, independence, and in some extreme cases, a threat to Spanish national unity. Decentralization, from this perspective, has been interpreted to undermine not only the Spanish state's authority over policy matters, but also reveals what some actors regard as the fragility of a united and democratic Spanish state. Actors' reflections on decentralization and regional-national relations often referred to past memories of the tenuous and dramatic shift towards democratization that ensued after the Francoist era.

Interviews with national educational system actors, their interpretations of "the regional" also remained locally focused on the autonomous community of Madrid. Reflecting on the complexity in relations between regional and national governments, one educational leader in the MEC explained that many of the national education policy made in relation to decentralization emanate from the local politics of the national Ministry and the regional government in Madrid. While the Socialist Party (PSOE) still leads the Spanish state government, the autonomous community of Madrid is governed by the Popular Party (PP). In relations between the national and regional governments in Madrid, education has become a deciding factor in the extent to which the state government decides to decentralize educational competencies to all regional governments nationwide, including Catalonia. One national policy maker explained,

In talking about schools...the Ministers have to make the decision that if they give more autonomy to the [regional] communities, the PP in Madrid will have more autonomy, so the schools where the Ministers send their children will be ran by the PP....Apparently, the Ministers are really trying to have it more centralized to prevent the PP from gaining more power in regional Madrid schools, which in turn affects all of the autonomies. (personal communication)

Adding to the complexity are the articulations of decentralization as a mechanism of cost-effectiveness.

Educational decentralization became a way for the Spanish state to reform the public sector that it inherited from the Francoist era, which was marked wholly by its absence in public education. As the Spanish state struggled to ease the financial burden of the increased educational demands of the mass (free and compulsory) educational system and the overhaul of public institutions inherited from the Francoist era, financial responsibilities were transferred to local and regional governments. This form of decentralization was advocated in response to global imperatives that ignited the need for national economies to draw upon local and regional strengths to meet the demands of the global economy. A model of economic growth promoted by the European Commission and OECD countries also influenced Spain.

Spain's accession into the EC in 1986 after years of negotiation involved a complete overhaul of its economy. After gaining EC membership, Spain pursued New Public Management (NPM) policies aligned with the interests of the EC in efficiency. This included a form of decentralization in order to enable Spain simultaneously to be able to meet the regional demands of some of the CCAA, like Catalonia and the Basque Country, and shift the economic burden of education onto the regions. Decentralization, for national level education system actors has been viewed as means of generating greater capital accumulation, giving the transfer of fiscal responsibilities to local and regional levels, while still maintaining central power over educational legislation. Furthermore, the Spanish state legitimizes itself through the use of decentralization policies as means of appearing to support regional and local concerns.

Interpretations of Europe

From the analysis presented in chapter 5, the EU has been constructed for both Spanish and Catalonia as a mechanism for the modernization of Spain politically, economically, and educationally. Yet, the ways in which central Spanish state actors interpret the EU show that it is still viewed both as a mediating and modernizing force, yet that it also is perceived as a contested space. The example of the establishment of regional offices in Brussels is one illustration of the national reaction to regional attempts to utilize the supranational space generated through the EU as means of bypassing and scale-jumping the nation state (Jessop, 1994).

For local and regional actors, however, the EU represents a forum in which to deepen a political form of decentralization. On the one hand, the EU represents a space of opportunity for Catalonia to push its agenda for greater self-governance. With an international presence gained through the EU, local and regional actors constructed the EU as an alternative power base that would deepen the decentralization process and provide the regional and local governments in Catalonia more autonomy over educational matters. Similarly, in Pereyra's (2002) interviews with system actors in Spain, local level actors argued that the current process of decentralization has needed an active external actor, such as the EU to coordinate education across and within Member State systems.

On the other hand, above all, the EU is a supranational organization of member states and EU policies are still generated through the jurisdiction of the Spanish national government. Catalonia is not considered an electoral constituency in Parliament elections, its language has not achieved status as an official language of the EU, and EU policies are still generated through the jurisdiction of the Spanish central government. Interviews with regional actors, who appeared to represent a more nationalist view of Catalan politics, perceived the EU as unwilling to meet their demands in each of these three areas. As stated by Roller (2004)

> demands like the creation of a single electoral constituency for European Parliament elections, the official recognition of representative offices in Brussels or direct access of regional authorities to the European Court of Justice have been ignored, much to the nationalists' frustration. (p. 94)

Moreover, as reflected by a number of regional educational leaders in Catalonia, there is a tension over the lack of EU economic support that Catalonia perceives has been occurring in relation to other CCAA in Spain. One educational authority in Catalonia reflected on EU Cohesion Funds that are distributed to the poorest and least developed regions in Europe.

While comparing the lack of these funds in Catalonia, which receives Objective 2 funds, with the economic development in Andalusia and Extremadura, which both receive Objective 1 funds, interpretations of national politics entered into the regional-EU discussion: "EU Cohesion Funds do not go to Catalonia, they go to Andalusia because it is a very poor region and they have always had good relations with the government in Madrid" (personal communication). Even as regional actors take into account what is happening at the EU level, national-regional tensions, and tensions between Catalonia and other CCAA are reflected. This demonstrates that policy is produced in a complex intersection of endogenous and exogenous forces which global-local hierarchical analysis and simple binary oppositional frameworks cannot illuminate. This also illustrates EU priorities for regions. The EU is largely an economic organizational and although Catalonia can assert regional matters onto supranational platform through the EU, the extent to which it is a central policy priority is connected to the purposes underlying the EU and how regional economic development fits within these purposes.

Similar to interviews with national actors, local and regional actors also appeared to be interpreting the EU as a source of pressure shaping education policy in new directions. From the perspective of local actors, the EU is "exercising great pressure" on education policy production through the promotion of a human capital framework of education (personal communication). At the local level, many of the actors made references to international comparative data being produced by the OECD, as well as Eurydice, the EU's network of educational indicators and other data. These comparative data were considered a "major source of motivation" to adopt policies and types of evaluation that yield greater "quality assurance" (personal communication). Global pressures in relation to new forms of international measurement in education were also taken into account at the local and regional levels.

In addition, since the reform of the democratic state, Catalonia and the other CCAA possess greater decision-making powers over particular policy areas compared to the centralized organization of the Francoist state. However, recent developments, including Spain's entry into what is today the EU and its negotiation of broader global processes, appear to have rearticulated the definition of decentralization to signify an administrative and fiscal conception of decentralization. As described in chapter 5, there is a strong anti-globalization movement in Spain that looks to press forward an alternative interpretation of globalization. At the local and regional level, EU policy agendas are interpreted as a neoliberal set of free market principals, and as a result, EU education policy have generated strong opposition at both the local and regional level. Consequently, from the perspective of local and regional actors in Catalonia, there is a preference to align with the rest of Spain on education policy issues than support EU policies, which are interpreted as means of pushing a neoliberal agenda in education and absorbing local, regional, and national heterogeneity into a converging global identity. The example of the protests staged in Barcelona against the Bologna Process is one illustration of the local and regional interpretation of EU and global processes. These multiple interpretations result in a complex set of debates out of which education policy emerge.

Chapter 5 showed that a European education policy space is actively informing educational discourses in Member State countries. EU educational programs have included the development of new policy instruments that align state policy according to international performance standards and benchmarks. With the new strategic objectives of Lisbon Strategy, the predominant emphases placed on education have been to facilitate lifelong learning, assume sound methods of quality assurance, and above all, aid in the development of a globally powerful knowledge-based economy. The OMC has become a central instrument in the establishment of benchmarks and performance indicators across educational systems of EU Member State countries.

As a powerful organization in the reshaping of education policy, the development of a European education policy space also has reconfigured educational governance and reshuffled the relationships between regions, nation states, and the EU. This is shown in the EU's promotion and rearticulation of decentralization as a key governance mechanism. While decentralization has been conceived as a bottom-up, grassroots approach of citizen empowerment, the EU advocates decentralization as means of economic integration and efficiency. This is aligned with global ideological discourses that support forms of administrative and fiscal decentralization, in which market efficiency is a primary concern. This is an uneasy and tenuous combination, at times easily aligned and at times explosive.

Over the past several decades of democracy in Spain, decentralization has been successively rearticulated to become more closely aligned with various policy pressures emerging from the EU and the broader global policy space. Although there are greater responsibilities, tasks, and funding allocations allotted to regional and local levels, this form of governance is typically employed in order to align regional and local priorities with what are perceived to be the imperatives of the global marketplace. In this way, regions are steered to follow particular policy agendas influenced by broader global processes. Ultimately, this has resulted in the marriage of Catalan identity politics, as indicated in a more politically-rooted form of decentralization, with a neoliberal form of globalization that, as part of its agenda, pushes to shift educational responsibilities, both administrative and fiscal to the regional and local levels.

European Policy Actors

In Europe, there are a number of tensions that extend across local, regional, and national. One educational leader explained that the Lisbon Strategy has placed extensive pressure on local, regional, and national levels to increase economic growth and social cohesion around the aims of the European integration project. The ways in which Europe conceives of its regions and local levels is linked to the EU's attempts to expand and deepen the European integration project. For the EU, regional governance has been promoted on the basis of leading to greater citizen participation in EU decision-making and thus, greater democratization. In education, this is supported by the principle of subsidiarity employed by the EU's decision-making institutions, which "gives precedence to lower territorial 'levels' of government over higher ones" (Anderson, 2001, p. 54). In addition, following the failure of the European Constitution in 2005, the EU has attempted to address issues of political legitimacy and deeply felt Euroskepticism. One of the ways that the EU has addressed these concerns is institutionally through an emphasis on its regions, local levels, and cities.

However, it must not be overlooked that the EU's primary interests have historically been economic. In this way, greater regional governance in the EU is promoted along the lines of greater economic integration in the EU. In an interview, an educational leader in Barcelona argued that the EU is "giving more money to regions and really promoting regional development" (personal communication). However, this participant went on to argue that although the EU emphasizes local and regional levels, "it is not the political and financial reality of Europe because the state still has a lot of power [because]…members of the EU are the states" (personal communication). In recent years, organizations, such as the OECD, World Bank, and the EU have promoted specific management and governance reforms, in which accountability, transparency, and decentralization are core practices of good governance. The pressures emanating from these organizations have shifted the definition of decentralization from political to a more administrative and financial form.

The EU specifically has referred to the need for education to meet demands of the knowledge-based global economy through the creation of flexible, innovative human capital. This has been increasingly emphasized since what is considered as the failure of the Lisbon objective. In the five years after the 2000 Lisbon objective, a new and more aggressive agenda has been established for education policy production. In recent policy shifts, there appears to be a sense of urgency regarding the failure of the Lisbon objective and the need to catch up with the US and Asia. This has the potential to deepen what Robertson (2007) called "a set of globally-oriented 'education' policies and programmes shaped by a new set of ideas about the production of a European knowledge economy" (p. 3). With a shift towards creating "a more open, globally-oriented, freer market Europe," policies produced in relation to educational governance will be more likely to advocate for administrative forms of decentralization in the name of efficiency (Robertson, 2007, p. 3).

Global pressures have influenced decentralization as means of economic efficiency, as well as a means of promoting local and regional identities as a form of resistance against what are perceived to be global homogenizing forces. At local, regional, and national levels, there are interpretations of the global as driving a particular set of pressures on education. These pressures often are conceived of as neoliberal policies aimed at greater economic efficiency and growth, increased human stock, and a deregulated state form, in which decentralization is a strategy of governance (Kamat, 2000). Moreover, broader global pressures have inspired a rearticulation of decentralization, underwritten by the belief that efficiency stems from less central bureaucracy.

For the EU, a particular interpretation of the global as inevitable and an economic imperative has become ingested and subsequently reflected in the post-Lisbon era. There is a new sense of urgency in EU policies that are looking to push for a freer market in order to generate economic growth on a competitive level with the US and Asia. This is markedly different than the EU's policy agenda in 2000, which represented a more optimistic vision of reaching the Lisbon objective (Robertson, 2007). With a greater sense of urgency for economic growth, decentralization for the EU is means of creating a free market, driven by means of market efficiency and capital accumulation. Both administrative and financial decentralization are advocated in order to spark efficiency, especially as these forms of decentralization are linked to broader notions of public management and/or good governance. While the EU emphasizes decentralization and regional decision-making to meet the goals of its European integration and economic expansion project, it remains to be seen whether in an era of global economic uncertainty, the EU is actually capable of successfully absorbing regional demands, and how the alignment of regional demands will blend with the economic and political aims of the EU, as well as nation states, such as Spain.

Thus far, this section has attempted to depict how rescaling processes are showing themselves as interactional across multiple scales through the shifting politics of decentralization. Moreover, this section has attempted to move beyond the hierarchical global to the local analysis often used to depict the impact of global processes on educational governance. Lastly, this section has raised a number of theoretical issues about how the state is conceived in contemporary debates of globalization. In relation to initial discussions of globalization and state theory, represented in chapter 2, the remainder of this chapter focuses on a reexamination of the state.

GLOBALIZING THE STATE IN EDUCATION POLICY

In recent years, critical geographers have shifted conceptions of the state in contemporary debates of globalization away from a view of state space as natural pre-given territorial and political demarcated state that divides intra- and inter-state relations (Brenner, Jessop, Jones, & MacLeod, 2003; Massey, 2005). Within contemporary debates about globalization, this has become increasingly significant, as globalization has "prompted social scientists to rethink issues of space, highlighting its social production and historical transformation in and through many emergent, interconnected geographical scales" (Brenner, Jessop, Jones, & MacLeod, 2003, p. 3). These authors went on to argue that

> Space no longer appears as a static platform or surface on which social relations are constructed, but rather as one of their constitutive dimensions. In particular the state's role as 'power container' appears to have been perforated; it seems to be leaking, and thus the inherited model of territorially self-enclosed, state-defined societies, economies, or cultures is becoming highly problematic. (Brenner, Jessop, Jones, & MacLeod, 2003, p. 3)

Global forces have been analyzed in this book in relation to state intervention in education, the reshaping of national policies, and new forms of governance produced in education.

This analysis has attempted to extend beyond the global-nation state duality and methodological nationalism too often used to examine the relationship between global forces, the state, and education policy formation. The dual analysis of the nation state and globalization relies too heavily on the assumption that either the state is sacrificed at the expense of globalization or globalization loses to the strong-state (Dale, 2005). Sassen (1996) aptly stated, "views that characterize the national state as simply losing significance fail to capture this very important fact and reduce what is happening to a function of the global-national duality: what one wins, the other loses" (p. 26). Furthermore, the theoretical position taken up in this book does not assume that all policies are being produced from within an end product of convergence, stemming from global pressures and neoliberal forces in education.

Rather, trends of divergence in how the state, market, and civil society of different systems negotiate particular global forces play a role as well. Bonal (2003) argued, "institutional factors play a crucial role in the form that 'globalisation' effects are recontextualized. The history of the education system, the articulation and strength of civil society, the state administrative and bureaucratic culture, etc., are possible divergence factors" (p. 160). Although citing pressures of neoliberalism, such as increased accountability and administrative forms of decentralization, it is not sufficient to argue that all state education systems are becoming privatized and in turn, handing over all that is public to the private. It is also inadequate to label a state formation as neoliberal, as if to suggest a completed project. Rather, these trends need to be conceptualized in such a way that allows us to see that education policy in a rescaled state is not a black and white transfer process, absent of actors, context, and history.

Across the multiscalar pressures that appear to be emanating from a complex network of actors from the local to the global, the binaries that dominate contemporary globalization literature are disrupted. In the context of analyses across chapters 4 and 5, the weak-state versus strong-state duality appears highly problematic, particularly as global processes and reconfigurations of the state are often varied, uneven, and highly contested. As evidenced in the case of Catalonia, Spain and the new Europe, more historically and politically rich perspectives on state transformation are needed in order to understand recent changes in education policy formation processes. As Held and McGrew (2002) argued, "globalization is a contingent historical process replete with conflicts and tensions" (p. 126). This account assumes that globalization is not a placeless, unipolar thing, happening everywhere in the same way at the same rate.

Rather, global processes are characteristically asymmetrical, in which "globalization is itself a deeply historical, uneven, and even *localizing* process" (Appadurai, 1996, p. 17). In other words, globalization does not necessarily have to be an either-or choice between the global and the local, convergence and divergence, order and disorder, integration and fragmentation (Robertson, 1992; Held & McGrew, 2003). Rather, as Mann (2003) pointed out, "what adds up to the global is a very complex mix of the local, the national, the inter-national...and the truly transnational" (p. 139). Put another way, globalization is a simultaneous set of processes "disorganize[ed] around the counterlogic of the *both/and*" (Wilson & Dissanayake, 1996, p. 8). With the emphasis on the ways in which actors at multiple levels engage with the interactions forming across scales highlights the process of globalization as much more than a set of structural processes and imperatives.

Burawoy et al. (2000) pointed out that one of the crucial dangers in viewing globalization solely as a set of forces is that they "will appear inevitable and natural" (p. 29). In many of the contemporary debates of globalization, even when globalization is conceived of as a process, it typically lacks an identification of "the subjects and drivers of the globalization process," and their particular implications, in this case, for education policy production (Dale & Robertson, 2002, p. 11). In other words, globalization remains a "process without a subject" (Hay, 1999). However, as argued in this book, global processes require analysis of how actors and agents at local, regional, national, supranational, and global scales are involved in shaping, negotiating, and implementing global pressures, forces, and imagination. This pushes an understanding of global forces as ideologically created, not pre-given and objective.

This book has shown that there is a need for more critical understandings of the ways in which the state is being reshaped, as well as how the state is reshaping itself in relation to global, supranational, regional, and local processes. Further, research is needed that seeks to adopt such a perspective in rejecting the thesis that the state no longer has a role to play, while accepting the state's role as reconfiguring. Geographical concepts of space and scale have been useful for alternative ways around the weak-state versus strong-state analyses within contemporary debates of globalization. Brenner, Jessop, Jones, and MacLeod

(2003) stated, "indeed, spatialized approaches to state restructuring have played a key role in facilitating the growing intellectual backlash among globalization researchers against naïve forecasts of the national state's imminent demise" (p. 4). From the case of Catalonia, Spain and Europe, it is maintained that the state is strategically being rescaled in relation to multiscalar forces and that although changed, the state continues to play a highly complex, significant role (Brenner, 2004; Dicken, 2003; Sassen, 1996).

The state is not static, but rather the state strategically shifts in order to manage the changing needs of the global economy and pressures emanating from regional and local scales. In the face of globalization,

> the position of the state [a]s being redefined in the context of a polycentric political-economic system in which national boundaries are more permeable than in the past. Nevertheless, the nation-state continues to contribute significantly towards the shaping and reshaping of the global economic map. (Dicken, 2003, p. 161)

From this theoretical perspective, the state is strategically reforming itself both in relation to supranational and global, as well as local, regional, and national imperatives and pressures.

Multiple, overlapping pressures have resulted in a multiscalar system of governance, in which local and regional institutions are increasingly engaged in policy production. Moreover, in exploring neoliberal pressures on education systems and the resulting shifts in education policy production, the state has been what Cerny (1990) has called the "competition state," what Ainley (2004) has cited as the "market-state," and others have labeled it the "neoliberal state" (Morrow & Torres, 2003). These conceptions suggest a completed project, when states are facing a multiplicity of diverse pressures. While states facing neoliberal pressures are often simply regarded as absent or hollowed-out, the Spanish state has in fact,

> morph[ed] into a variety of institutional forms, to insinuate itself into, and graft itself onto, a range of different institutional settlements, and to absorb parallel and even contending narratives of restructuring and intervention, in response both to internal contradictions and external pressures. (Tickell & Peck, 2002, p. 23)

The dynamic reinvention of the Spanish state stands against the grain of functionalist arguments about global pressures, neoliberalism, and the absentee state.

The literature on education policy production in relation to decentralization often has relied upon a linear, hierarchical process from the global to the local and the local to the global. Theoretically, these issues often are conceptualized with terms such as top-town, bottom-up, margin-center, center-periphery. Conceptions such as these, and of global-nation state suggest an exclusive territorial and political national state space. They represent

> maps [that] depict a plethora of distinct state territories, large and small, demarcated as color-coded 'blocks' of space on a flat surface. Thus each individual state is represented as a *kind of container* that separates an 'inside'

of domestic political interactions from an 'outside' of international or inter-state relations. (Brenner, Jessop, Jones, & MacLeod, 2003, p. 1; my emphasis)

From reflections generated from the individual human actors involved in the interpretation, negotiation and production of education policy, these theoretical conceptions appear to be becoming quickly exhausted.

The case of study of Catalonia, Spain and the new Europe presented in this book, as they have shifted in the 21st century, globalized world pushes for a more nuanced and complex view of the politics of education policy of decentralization. Related to these two points is the articulation and rearticulation of decentralization, which is being done by a whole range of actors at multiple scales. When actors are brought to the forefront of studies of policy production, and attention is brought to the ways in which these actors are engaging with pressures emanating from multiple scales, perspectives are gained on the ways in which processes of decentralization and nation state rescaling are being actively struggled over in policy terms.

CONCLUSION

This final section of this chapter attempts to summarize and tie together the key arguments and ideas presented in this book as a way of conclusion. Within contemporary debates about globalization, much of the research has showcased the transformation of the nation state, including the ways in which globalization has reshaped national educational systems around the world. Studies of this kind often have presupposed the production of education policy from within a sealed off and depoliticized space, in which the nation state has exclusive authority. Extending beyond dominant binary oppositions that uphold both state-centrism and methodological nationalism, this book has sought to show how education policy is actively being produced in relation to a range of multiple pressures and sources.

This book has attempted to move beyond the state-centric views of policy to focus on how policy actors actually negotiate local and regional imperatives, as well as ideas emanating from the central Spanish government, a developing European agenda, and notions circulating within the global space. These policy ideas and imperatives have divergent orientations, such as to increase system efficiency, to expand opportunities for greater educational equity and equality, or pressures emanating from the historical and political tensions between Catalonia and the central Spanish state over issues of educational autonomy. By looking at the overlap and interaction of education policy actors and arenas, this book has attempted to map out the spatial and temporal impact of these multiple considerations on education policy production, particularly those related to educational decentralization as a form of nation state rescaling.

The perspective on education policy taken up in this book is one focused on the front-end stages of policy pressures, negotiation, and production, drawing primarily on the experiences and perspectives of actors at local, regional, national, and supranational levels. By foregrounding the agency of policy actors engaged in the production, interpretation, and articulation of policy pressures, education policy formation is not fixed and objective, but rather a complex, contested, and debated set of processes. By engaging the messiness of policy production processes, it appears that education policy is unlike any other area of social policy, in the perspectives gained on globalization, regionalization and shifts in the nation state.

From this perspective, this book has shown that the changing territorial shape and shifting political and economic organization of the Spanish state has resulted in a complex division of educational competencies between the central state and Catalonia. Against the development of a European education policy space, in combination with new regionalisms, the Spanish education system is situated within a complex, multilateral crossfire of diverse and often contrasting aims of education. This has major implications for the ways in which educational decentralization, and more broadly, governance, needs to be conceptualized beyond frameworks and models, which uphold state-centrism and methodological nationalism. In relation to these reflections, this book has suggested the conceptual importance of scale and rescaling to illuminate the reconfiguration of the state and new modes of governance produced in education.

In this book, it has been the underlying aim to illustrate the case of educational policy formation in Catalonia not from within binary opposition or global-local hierarchical frameworks that seem to dominate the globalization literature, but rather from a perspective of the state as constantly in flux, facing complex, and at times contrasting pressures. The analyses drawn from this study reveal that the state is strategically being reconfigured in relation to multiscalar forces, and these reconfigurations of the state appear to be varied, uneven, and highly contested. However, although changed, the state continues to play a highly complex, significant role.

The concept of rescaling is particularly useful in showing that the state is not static, as it is conceived in some of the literature on globalization, but rather the role of the state in education policy production is strategically reforming itself both in relation to supranational and global, as well as local, regional, and national imperatives and pressures. Yet, what this project also has illustrated is that rescaling, albeit useful for considering contemporary shifts in state space, cannot be understood without first considering the particular actors that are involved in negotiating and producing scale.

As evidenced in this project, more historically and politically rich perspectives on state transformation are needed in order to understand recent changes in policy production processes. These perspectives allow for a more critical understanding of the ways in which the state is being reshaped, as well as how the state is reshaping itself in relation to global, supranational, regional, and local processes. These reflections on globalization and state theory have been illustrated in this book through multiple and rearticulated conceptions of policy focused on educational decentralization. Over the past thirty years in Spain, educational decentralization has emerged as a central process to the emergence of a new democratic Spanish state. This conception of decentralization was aligned with a more political form of devolution focused on regional empowerment of the CCAA and greater democratization.

However, policy concepts surrounding educational decentralization are not only formed in relation to national-local dynamics but are influenced more broadly by a complex set of regional and global considerations. Over the past thirty years, the politics of decentralization have been successively rearticulated to become more closely aligned with various policy pressures emerging from the EU and the broader global policy space to utilize education as a way to ensure efficiency, productivity, and economic growth. In the post-Lisbon era in the EU, with an increasing sense of urgency to develop policies aimed to inspire and spark greater EU economic growth, this appears to be influential on new modes of governance produced, in which functional and financial decentralization is a central mechanism.

The aims of this book were not to give a set of definitive answers or future predictions. Rather, this book aimed to problematize some of the dominant frameworks and models utilized in the study of globalization, nation state reformation, education policy, and educational governance. While further empirical work is required to better understand the ways in which national systems of education are shaped by global processes, this book suggests that globalization can no longer be conceptualized as a homogenous, standardizing force and that education policy can no longer be conceived as being produced in a self-contained, depoliticized space. Rather, education policy production is and will continue to be influenced and produced in relation to inputs arising from a range of sources. Within these spaces of friction that continue to emerge as a result of globalization, the interaction and clash of regional, national and supranational education policy priorities will not likely relent in the future. In order to critically engage these education policy formation processes and to be able to rethink the key educational concepts underlying these processes, we require new frameworks and models for understanding state formations in education policy in the global era.

REFERENCES

Ainley, P. (2004). The new 'market-state' and education. *Journal of Education Policy, 19*(4), 497–514.

Alexander, N. C. (2002). *Paying for education: How the world bank & IMF influence education in developing countries.* Retrieved May 22, 2006, from http://www.servicesforall.org/html/otherpubs/Paying_For_Education2002.pdf

Almódovar, P. (Producer/Writer/Director). (1983). *La flor de mi secreto* [The flower of my secret]. [Motion Picture]. El Deseo, S.A.

Amin, S. (1980). The class structure of the contemporary imperialist system. *Monthly Review, 31*(8), 9–26.

Anderson, B. (1983). *Imagined communities: Reflections on the origins and spread of nationalism.* London: Verso.

Anderson, J. (2001). The rise of regions and regionalism in Western Europe. In M. Guibernau (Ed.), *Governing European diversity* (pp. 35–64). London: Sage.

Appadurai, A. (1996). *Modernity at large: Cultural dimensions of globalization.* Minneapolis: University of Minnesota Press.

Applegate, C. (1999). A Europe of regions: Reflections on the historiography of regional places in modern times. *The American Historical Review, 104*(4), 1–32.

Aribau i Farriols, B. C. (1832). *Oda a la pàtria* [Ode to the country]. Barcelona, Spain.

Aroca, J. V. (2006, June 19). Maragall llama a todos a integrarse en el sí [Maragall calls on everyone to vote yes]. *La Vanguardia*, 17.

Astiz, F. M., Wiseman, A. W., & Baker, D. P. (2002). Slouching towards decentralization: Consequences of globalization for curricular control in national education systems. *Comparative Education Review, 46*(1), 66–86.

Balcells, A. (1996). *Catalan nationalism: Past and present.* New York: St. Martin's Press.

Bale, T. (2005). *European politics: A comparative introduction.* London: Palgrave Macmillan.

Balfour, S. (2005). The popular party since 1989. In S. Balfour (Ed.), *The politics of contemporary Spain* (pp. 146–168). London: Routledge.

Ball, S. (1990). *Politics and policy making in education: Explorations in policy sociology.* London: Routledge.

Ball, S. (1994). *Educational reform: A critical and post-structural approach.* Buckingham, England: Open University Press.

Barber, B. (1996). *Jihad versus McWorld: Terrorism's challenge to democracy.* New York: Ballantine Books.

Bauman, Z. (1998). *Globalization: The human consequences.* Oxford: Polity.

Becker, G. (1964). *Human capital.* New York: National Bureau of Economic Research.

Benyon, J., & Dunkerley, D. (2000). What is globalization? In J. Benyon & D. Dunkerly (Eds.), *Globalization: The reader* (pp. 3–13). New York: Routledge.

Berman, E. H., Marginson, S., Preston, R., McClellan, B. E., & Arnove, R. F. (2003). The political economy of educational reform in Australia, England and Wales, and the United States. In R. F. Arnove & C. A. Torres (Eds.), *Comparative education: The dialectic of the global and the local* (pp. 252–291). Oxford, England: Rowman & Littlefield Publishers.

Biesta, J. (2004). Education, accountability, and the ethical demand: Can the democratic potential of accountability be regained? *Educational Theory, 54*(3), 233–250.

Blackmore, J. (2000). Globalization: A useful concept for feminists rethinking theory and strategies in education? In N. Burbules & C. A. Torres (Eds.), *Globalization and education: Critical perspectives* (pp. 133–155). London: Routledge.

Blitz, B. (2003). From Monnet to Delors: Educational co-operation in the European Union. *Contemporary European History, 12*(2), 1–16.

REFERENCES

Bonal, X. (1998). La política educativa: Dimensiones de un proceso de transformación (1976–1996) [Education policy: Dimensions of a process of transformation (1976–1996)]. In R. Goma & J. Subirats (Eds.), *Políticas públicas en España: Contenidos, redes de actores y niveles de gobierno* [Public policy in Spain: Issues, networks of actors and levels of government] (pp. 153–175). Editorial Ariel, S.A.

Bonal, X. (2000). Interest groups and the State in contemporary Spanish education policy. *Journal of Education Policy, 15*(2), 201–216.

Bonal, X. (2003). The neoliberal educational agenda and the legitimation crisis: Old and new state strategies. *British Journal of Sociology of Education, 24*(2), 159–175.

Bonal, X., & Rambla, X. (1996). La política educative a Catalunya: universalització, fragmentació i reproducció de les desigualtats [Education policy in Catalonia: Universalization, fragmentation, and reproduction of inequalities]. In R. Goma & J. Subirats (Eds.), *Govern i polítiques públiques a Catalunya (1980–2000): Autonomia I benestar* [Government and public policy in Catalonia (1980–2000): Autonomy and well-being]. Universitat Autònoma de Barcelona: Servei de Publicacions.

Borrás-Alomar, S., Christiansen, T., & Rodríguez-Pose, A. (1994). Towards a 'Europe of the Regions'? Visions and reality from a critical perspective. *Regional Politics and Policy, 4*(2), 1–27.

Borrás, S., & Jacobsson, K. (2004). The open method of co-ordination and new governance patterns in the EU. *Journal of European Public Policy, 11*(2), 185–208.

Börzel, T. A. (2002). *States and regions in the European Union: Institutional adaptation in Germany and Spain.* Cambridge, England: Cambridge University Press.

Brassloff, A. (1996). Centre-periphery communication in Spain: The politics of language and the language of politics. In C. Hoffman (Ed.), *Language, culture and communication in contemporary Europe* (pp. 111–123). Clevedon, England: Multilingual Matters Ltd.

Bray, M. (1999). Control of education: Issues and tensions in centralization and decentralization. In R. F. Arnove & C. A. Torres (Eds.), *Comparative education: The dialectic of the global and the local* (pp. 204–227). Oxford, England: Rowman and Littlefield Publishers.

Bray, M., & Mukundan, M. V. (2003). *Management and governance for EFA: Is decentralisation really the answer?* Retrieved May 20, 2006, from www.hku.hk/cerc

Brenner, N. (2001). The limits to scale? Methodological reflections on scalar structuration. *Progress in Human Geography, 25*(4), 591–614.

Brenner, N. (2004). *New state spaces: Urban governance and the rescaling of statehood.* Oxford, England: Oxford University Press.

Brenner, N., & Theodore, N. (Eds.). (2002). *Spaces of neoliberalism: urban restructuring in North America and Western Europe.* Oxford: Blackwell Publishing.

Brenner, N., Jessop, B., Jones, M., & MacLeod, G. (Eds.). (2003). *State/Space: A reader.* Oxford, England: Blackwell.

Bresso, M. (2006, Autumn). The regions and the future of Europe in the constitution. *Social Europe: The Journal of the European Left, 2*(2), 64–67.

Burawoy, M., Blum, J., George, S., Gille, Z., Gowan, T., Haney, L., et al. (Eds.). (2000). *Global ethnography: Forces, connections, and imaginations in a postmodern world.* Berkeley, CA: University of California Press.

Burbules, N., & Torres, C. (Eds.). (2000). *Globalization and critical perspectives.* London: Routledge.

Calero, J. (2005, April). *Thematic review. Equity in education: Country analytical report—Spain.* OECD Publishing: Center for Educational Research and Innovation.

Calhoun, C. (2004). The democratic integration of Europe: Interests, identity and the public sphere. *Eurozine.* Retrieved July 15, 2004, from http://www.eurozine.com/article/2004-06-21-calhoun-en.html

Carrajo, M. (1993). Education and training. In A. Almarcha Barbado (Ed.), *Spain and EC membership evaluated* (pp. 179–194). New York: St. Martin's Press.

Castells, M. (1996). *The rise of the network society.* Oxford, England: Blackwell.

Cerny, P. G. (1990). *Changing architecture of politics: Structure, agency and the future of the state.* London: Sage.

Closa, C., & Heywood, P. M. (2004). *Spain and the European Union*. London: Palgrave Macmillan.

Cohen, R., & Kennedy, P. (2000). *Global sociology*. New York: New York University Press.

Constitución Española [Spanish Constitution]. (1978). Retrieved March 1, 2007, from http://www.congreso.es/funciones/constitucion/indice.htm

Corner, T. (1988). The maritime and border regions of Western Europe. *Comparative Education, 24*(2), 229–245.

Council of the European Union. (2007, July). *Brussels European council: Presidential conclusions*. Retrieved May 15, 2009, from http://www.consilium.europa.eu/ueDocs/cms_Data/docs/pressData/en/ec/94932.pdf

Cowen, R. (2003). Comparing futures or comparing pasts? In E. Beauchamp (Ed.), *Comparative education reader* (pp. 3–16). New York: Routledge.

Dale, R. (2000). Globalization and education: Demonstrating a 'common world educational culture' or locating a 'globally structured educational agenda'? *Educational Theory, 50*(4), 419–427.

Dale, R. (2004). Forms of governance, governmentality and the EU's open method of coordination. In W. Larner & W. Walters (Eds.), *Global governmentality: Governing international spaces* (pp. 174–194). London: Routledge.

Dale, R. (2005). Globalisation, knowledge economy and comparative education. *Comparative Education, 41*(2), 117–149.

Dale, R., & Robertson, S. (2002). The varying effects of supranational organizations as subjects of globalization on education. *Comparative Education Review, 46*(1), 10–36.

Daryl Slack, J. (1996). The theory and method of articulation in cultural studies. In D. Morley & D. K. Chen (Eds.), *Stuart Hall: Critical dialogues in cultural studies* (pp. 113–129). New York: Routledge.

De la Caba Collado, M., & López Atxurra, R. (2006). Democratic citizenship in textbooks in Spanish primary curriculum. *Journal of Curriculum Studies, 38*(2), 205–228.

Dicken, P. (2003). *Global shift: Reshaping the global economic map in the 21st century* (4th ed.). New York: Guilford Press.

Dror, Y. (1968). *Public policymaking reexamined*. Scranton, PA: Chandler.

Easton, D. (1965). *A framework for political analysis*. Englewood Cliffs, NJ: Prentice-Hall.

Edge, K. (2000). *Spain's democratization & decentralization reform*. Report prepared for the Education Reform and Management Group, HDNED, World Bank. Retrieved February 7, 2006, from http://www1.worldbank.org/education/globaleducationreform/06.GovernaceReform/06.05.casestudies/spainof.html#CaseStudies

Engel, L. C. (2007a). *Rescaling the state: The politics of educational decentralization in Catalonia*. Doctoral dissertation, University of Illinois at Urbana-Champaign, USA.

Engel, L. C. (2007b). Policy as journey: Tracing the steps of a reinvented Spanish state. In C. McCarthy, A. S. Durham, L. C. Engel, A. A. Filmer, M. D. Giardina, & M. A. Malagreca (Eds.), *Globalizing cultural studies: Ethnographic interventions in theory, method, and policy* (pp. 385–406). New York: Peter Lang.

Engel, L. C., & Ortloff, D. H. (2009). From the local to the supranational: Curriculum reform and the production of the ideal citizen in two federal systems, German and Spain. *Journal of Curriculum Studies, 41*(2), 179–198.

España 2000. (n.d.). Retrieved March 8, 2007, from http://www.esp2000.org/v3/

Esturla, A. (2000). Spain. In C. Brock & W. Tulasiewicz (Eds.), *Education in a single Europe* (pp. 321–343). New York: Routledge.

European Commission. (n.d.). *Treaty establishing the European coal and steel community, ECSC Treaty*. Retrieved May 12, 2009, from http://europa.eu/scadplus/treaties/ecsc_en.htm

European Commission. (n.d.). *Treaty of Lisbon: Taking European into the 21st century*. Retrieved May 12, 2009, from http://europa.eu/lisbon_treaty/glance/index_en.htm

European Commission. (1983). *Accession criteria: Copenhagen European council*. Retrieved March 15, 2007, from http://ec.europa.eu/enlargement/enlargement_process/accession_process/criteria/index_en.htm

REFERENCES

European Commission. (1992). *Treaty on European Union.* Retrieved May 17, 2009, from http://eur-lex.europa.eu/en/treaties/dat/11992M/htm/11992M.html#0001000001

European Commission. (1994). *White paper: Growth, competitiveness, employment.* Luxembourg: Office for Official Publications of the European Communities.

European Commission. (1996). *White paper: Teaching and learning—towards a learning society.* Luxembourg: Office for Official Publications of the European Communities.

European Commission. (2000a). *Working for the regions* [Brochure]. Luxembourg: Office for Official Publications of the European Communities.

European Commission. (2000b, March). *Presidential conclusions: Lisbon European Council.* Retrieved February 2, 2006, from http://www.europarl.europa.eu/summits/lis1_en.htm#a. Accessed on 6 November 2007.

European Commission. (2002). *European benchmarks in education and training.* Retrieved February 15, 2006, from http://europa.eu/scadplus/leg/en/cha/c11064.htm

European Communities. (2004). *A constitution for Europe.* Luxembourg: Office for Official Publications of the European Communities.

European Commission. (2007, February). *Communication from the Commission: A coherent framework of indicators and benchmarks for monitoring progress towards the Lisbon objectives in education and training.* Retrieved March 20, 2007, from http://eur-lex.europa.eu/LexUriServ/site/en/com/2007/com2007_0061en01.pdf

Eurydice. (2005). *Citizenship education at school in Europe: Spain: National description, 2004/05* (Brussels: European Commission, Eurydice European Unit). Retrieved October 7, 2008, from http://eacea.ec.europa.eu/ressources/eurydice/pdf/054DN/054_ES_EN.pdf.

Eurydice. (2008). *The education system in Spain, 2007/08.* Eurybase: The Information Database on Education Systems in Europe (Brussels: European Commission), 1–32. Retrieved October 8, 2008, from http://eacea.ec.europa.eu/ressources/eurydice/eurybase/pdf/0_integral/ES_EN.pdf.

Farrell, M. (2005). Spain the new European Union: In search of a new role and identity. In S. Balfour (Ed.), *The politics of contemporary Spain* (pp. 215–234). New York: Routledge.

Ferrer, F. (2000). Languages, minorities and education in Spain: The case of Catalonia. *Comparative Education, 36*(2), 187–197.

Fierro, A. (1994). Diseño y desafíos de la reforma educativa española [Design and challenges of the Spanish education reform]. *Revista de Educación* [Journal of Education], *305,* 13–36.

Fiske, E. B. (1996). *Decentralization of education: Politics and consensus.* Washington, DC: World Bank.

Forster, A., & Wallace, W. (2000). Common foreign and security policy. In H. Wallace & W. Wallace (Eds.), *Policy-making in the European Union* (4th ed., pp. 461–491). Oxford, England: Oxford University Press.

Frank, A. G. (1998). *ReOrient: Global economy in the Asian age.* Berkeley, CA: University of California Press.

Fraser, R. (1994). *Blood of Spain: An oral history of the Spanish civil war.* London: Pimlico.

Generalitat de Catalunya. (1983). *Llei de Normalizació Lingüística del Catalá* [Catalan Language Normalization Law]. Barcelona: Departament de la Presidéncia.

Generalitat de Catalunya. (1998). *Ley de Política Lingüística 1/1998 de 7 de enero* [Law 1/1998 of January 7, of Linguistic Policy]. Barcelona: Departament de la Presidéncia.

Generalitat de Catalunya. (2002). *Catalan, a European language* [Brochure]. Barcelona, Spain: Departament de Cultura.

Generalitat de Catalunya. (2003). *Informe sobre la reforma del estatuto.* Report on the reform of the Statute. Barcelona, Spain: Departament de Governació i Relacions Institucionals; Institut d'Estudis Autonomics.

Generalitat de Catalunya. (2004, December). *Estudi PISA 2003 avançament de resultats* [PISA 2003 advancement of results]. Barcelona, Spain: Departament d'Educació.

Generalitat de Catalunya. (2005a). *Pacte Nacional per a l'Educació oportunitat i compromís: Idees per al debat* [National Pact for educational opportunity and compromise: Ideas for the debate]. Barcelona, Spain: Departament d'Educació.

Generalitat de Catalunya. (2005c). *Proposal for a new statute of autonomy.* Retrieved April 28, 2006, from http://www.gencat.net/nourestatut/es/index_es.htm

Generalitat de Catalunya. (2006a). *Estatut d'autonomia de Catalunya: Proposta sotmesa a referéndum el dia 18 de juny de 2006* [Statute of Autonomy of Catalonia: Proposal for the referendum on June 18, 2006]. Barcelona, Spain: Departament de la Presidéncia.

Generalitat de Catalunya. (2006b). *Pacte Nacional per a l'Educació* [National Pact for Education]. Barcelona, Spain: Departament d'Educació.

Generalitat de Catalunya. (2006c). *Statute of autonomy.* Retrieved June 27, 2006, from http://www.gencat.cat/generalitat/eng/estatut/titol_preliminar.htm

Giddens, A. (1999). The runaway world. *BBC Reith lectures.* Retrieved December 9, 2004, from http://news.bbc.co.uk/hi/english/static/events/reith_99/default.htm

Gillespie, R. (2000). *Spain and the Mediterranean: Developing a European policy towards the south.* London: Macmillan Press.

Giordano, B., & Roller, E. (2002). Catalonia and the 'Idea of Europe': Competing strategies and discourses within Catalan party politics. *European Urban and Supranational Studies, 9*(2), 99–113.

Gisbert, J. (2006, May 23). CiU aprovechará el referéndum del Estatut para explicar su programa de gobierno para Catalunya [CiU will take advantage of the referéndum of the Statute in order to explain its government program for Catalonia]. *La Vanguardia,* 20.

Gorostiaga Derqui, J. M. (2001). Educational decentralization policies in Argentina and Brazil: Exploring new trends. *Journal of Education Policy, 16*(6), 561–583.

Grant, N. (1988). The education of minority and peripheral cultures: Introduction. *Comparative Education, 24*(2), 155–166.

Green, A. (1997). *Education, globalization and the nation state.* London: Macmillan Press.

Guibernau, M. (1999). *Nations without states: Political communities in a global age.* Cambridge, England: Polity Press.

Guibernau, M. (2006). Nations without states in the EU: The Catalan case. In J. McGarry & M. Keating (Eds.), *European integration and the nationalities question* (pp. 216–224). London: Routledge.

Guillén, A. M., & Álvarez, S. (2001). Globalization and the southern welfare states. In R. Sykes, B. Palier, & P. M. Prior (Eds.), *Globalization and European welfare states: Challenges and change* (pp. 103–126). New York: Palgrave.

Hall, S., & duGay, P. (1996). *Questions of cultural identity.* London: Sage.

Ham, C., & Hill, M. (1993). *The policy process in the modern capitalist state.* New York: Harvester Wheatsheaf.

Hanson, M. E. (1989a). Decentralisation and regionalisation in educational administration: Comparisons of Venezuela, Colombia and Spain. *Comparative Education, 25*(1), 41–55.

Hanson, M. E. (1989b). Education, administration development and democracy in Spain. *International Journal of Educational Development, 9*(2), 127–138.

Hanson, M. E. (1998). Strategies of educational decentralization: Key questions and core issues. *Journal of Educational Administration, 36*(2), 111–128.

Hanson, M. E. (2000). Democratization and educational decentralization in Spain. *Education Reform and Management Country Study Series.* Washington, DC: World Bank.

Hartley, D. (2003). Education as a global positioning device: Some theoretical considerations. *Comparative Education, 39*(4), 439–450.

Harvey, D. (1989). *The condition of postmodernity.* Oxford, England: Blackwell.

Harvey, D. (2005). *A brief history of neoliberalism.* Oxford: Oxford University Press.

Hay, C. (1999, December). *What place for ideas in the structure-agency debate? Globalization as a process without a subject.* Paper presented at the annual conference of the British International Studies Association, University of Manchester, England.

Hay, J. (2003). The (neo)liberalization of the domestic sphere and the new architecture of community. In J. Z. Bratich, J. Packer, & C. McCarthy (Eds.), *Foucault, cultural studies, and governmentality* (pp. 165–206). New York: State University of New York Press.

Held, D., & McGrew, A. (2002). *Globalization/Anti-globalization.* Cambridge, England: Polity Press.

REFERENCES

Held, D., & McGrew, A. (Eds.). (2003). *The global transformation reader: An introduction to the globalization debate*. Cambridge, England: Polity Press.

Henry, M., Lingard, B., Rizvi, F., & Taylor, S. (2000). *The OECD, globalization and education policy*. Oxford, England: Pergamon Press.

Hens, M. (2007, January 7). Catalans grapple with migrant influx. *BBC News*. Retrieved January 20, 2007, from http://news.bbc.co.uk

Heywood, P. (1995). *The government and politics of Spain*. New York: St. Martin's Press.

High Level Group. (2004). *Facing the challenge: The Lisbon strategy for growth and employment*. Report from the High Level Group chaired by Wim Kok. Luxembourg: Office for Official Publications of the European Communities.

Hingel, A. J. (2001, March). *Education policies and educational governance*. Brussels, Belgium: European Commission.

Hirst, P. Q., & Thompson, G. (1996). *Globalization in question*. Cambridge, England: Polity Press.

Holford, J. (2008). Hard measures for soft stuff: Citizenship indicators and educational policy under the Lisbon strategy. *European Educational Research Journal, 7*(3), 331–343.

Holman, O. (1996). *Integrating southern Europe: EC expansion and the transnationalization of Spain*. London: Routledge.

Hood, C. (1991). A public management for all seasons. *Public Administration, 69*, 3–19.

Hughes, R. (1993). *Barcelona*. New York: Vintage, Random House Inc.

Huntington, S. (1996). *Clash of civilizations and the remaking of world order*. New York: Simon and Schuster.

International Monetary Fund. (2009, April). *World economic outlook database*. Retrieved May 15, 2009, from http://www.imf.org/

Iriye, A. (2004). *Global community: The role of international organizations in the making of the contemporary world*. Berkley, CA: University of California Press.

Jacott, L., & Maldonado Rico, A. (2006). The *Centros Concertados* in Spain, parental demand and implications for equity. *European Journal of Education, 41*(1), 97–111.

Jeffery, C. (2002). Social and supranational interests: ESC and Committee of the Regions. In J. Peterson & M. Shackleton (Eds.), *The Institutions of the European Union* (pp. 326–346). Oxford, England: Oxford University Press.

Jessop, B. (1994). Post-Fordism and the state. In A. Amin (Ed.), *Post-Fordism: A reader* (pp. 251–279). Cambridge, MA: Blackwell.

Jessop, B. (1999). The changing governance of welfare: Recent trends in its primary functions, scale and modes of coordination. *Social Policy and Administration, 33*(4), 348–359.

Jones, B., & Keating, M. (Eds.). (1995). *The European Union and the regions*. Oxford, England: Oxford University Press.

Jones, P. W. (1998). Globalisation and internationalism: Democratic prospects.... *Comparative Education, 34*(2), 143–155.

Jones, R. (2000). *Beyond the Spanish state: Central government, domestic actors and the EU*. New York: Palgrave.

Jou, L., & Meliá, J. (2002). El català I l'Any Europeu de les Llengues [Catalan and the European Year of Languages]. *Llengua I ús: Revista técnica de politica lingüística* [Language and use: Technical journal of language policy], *23*, 4–11.

Kamat, S. (2000). Deconstructing the rhetoric of decentralization: The state in education reform. *Current Issues in Comparative Education, 2*(2), 1–9.

Karlsen, G. E. (2000). Decentralized centralism: Framework for a better understanding of governance in the field of education. *Journal of Education Policy, 15*(5), 525–538.

Karlsen, G. E. (2002). Educational policy and educational programmes in the European Union. In J. Ibáñez-Martín & G. Jover (Eds.), *Education in Europe: Policies and politics* (pp. 23–49). London: Kluwer Academic Publishers.

Keating, M. (1995). Europeanism and regionalism. In B. Jones & M. Keating (Eds.), *The European Union and the regions* (pp. 1–19). Oxford, England: Oxford University Press.

Kellas, J. G. (2004). *Nationalist politics in Europe: The Constitutional and electoral dimensions*. New York: Palgrave.

Kelsey, J. (1995). *The New Zealand experiment: A world model for structural adjustment*. Auckland, New Zealand: Auckland University Press.

Kenway, J., & Fahey, J. (2009). *Globalising the research imagination*. New York: Routledge.

Kivinen, O., & Nurmi, J. (2003). Unifying higher education for different kinds of Europeans. Higher education and work: A comparison of ten countries. *Comparative Education, 39*(1), 83–103.

Larsson, A. (2002, March). *The new open method of co-ordination: A sustainable way between a fragmented Europe and a European supra state: A practioner's view*. Lecture, Uppsala University.

Lawn, M. (2006). Soft governance and the learning spaces of Europe. *Comparative European Politics, 4*, 272-288.

Lawn, M. & Lingard, B. (2002). Constructing a European policy space in educational governance: The role of transnational policy actors. *European Educational Research Journal, 1(2)*, 290-307.

Local Government International Bureau. (2005, June). *Committee of the regions*. Retrieved May 2, 2005, from http://international.lga.gov.uk/representation/cor/index.html

Lodge, M. (2005). The importance of being modern: International benchmarking and national regulatory innovation. *Journal of European Public Policy, 12*(4), 649–667.

López, R. A. (2006). De la LOCE a la LOE: las respuestas del a LOE [From the LOCE to the LOE: Responses of the LOE]. *Religión y Escuela* [Religion and School], 14–16.

Lugg, C. A. (1997). *Crossing borders in a media driven age: The rise of "PRolicy"*. Paper presented at the annual meeting of the University Council for Educational Administration.

MacLennan, J. C. (2000). *Spain and the process of European integration, 1957–85*. New York: Palgrave.

MacLeod, G. (1999). Place, politics, and scale dependence: Exploring the structuration of Euro-supranationalism. *European Urban and Supranational Studies, 6*, 231–253.

Mann, M. (2003). Has globalization ended the rise and rise of the nation-state? In D. Held & A. McGrew (Eds.), *The global transformations reader: An introduction to the globalization debate* (pp. 135–146). Cambridge, England: Polity Press.

Maragall, J. (1981). *Antologia poètica* [Poetic anthology]. Barcelona, Spain: Edicions, 62.

Marginson, S. (1999). After globalization: Emerging politics of education. *Journal of Education Policy, 14*(1), 19–31.

Marston, S. A., & Smith, N. (2001). States, scales and households: limits to scale thinking? A response to Brenner. *Progress in Human Geography, 25*(4), 615–619.

Martín, C. M. (2006, March). La evaluación del sistema educativo [The evaluation of the education system]. *Revista de Educación: PISA* [Journal of Education: PISA] (pp. 315–336). Madrid, Spain: INECSE.

Martins, H. (1974). Time and theory in sociology. In J. Rex (ed.). *Approaches to sociology: An introduction to major trends in British sociology* (pp. 246-294). London: Routledge.

Maset, J. P. (2006, May 27). Crecen las desigualdades en la escuela catalana [Inequalities grow in the Catalan school]. *La Vanguardia, 36*.

Massey. D. (2005). *For space*. London: Sage.

Mauter, W. (1998). Churchill and the unification of Europe. *The Historian, 61*(1), 67–84.

McCarthy, C., Durham, A. S., Engel, L. C., Filmer, A. A., Giardina, M. D., & Malagreca, M. A. (Eds.). *Globalizing cultural studies: Ethnographic interventions in theory, method, and policy*. New York: Peter Lang.

Mead, N. (2006, March). Constitutional furor: The proposed Estatut has generated plenty of controversy, but it's not done yet. *Barcelona Metropolitan*, 16–18.

Ministerio de Educación y Ciencia. (MEC). (n.d.). *¿Qué es la Alta Inspección?* Retrieved February 2, 2007, from http://www.mec.es/educa/jsp/plantilla.jsp?area=ccaa&id=31

Ministerio de Educación y Ciencia. (MEC). (1999, September-December). *Revista de educación 320: La Inspección Educativa* [Journal of Education 320: Educational inspection]. Madrid: INCE.

REFERENCES

Ministerio de Educación y Cieneia. (MEC). (2002, December 23). Disposiciones generales: Jefatura del Estado. Ley Organica 10/2002, de 23 de diciembre, de Calidad de la Educación.

Ministerio de Educación y Ciencia. (MEC). (2006, May 3). Disposiciones generales: Jefatura del Estado. Ley Organica 2/2006, de 3 de mayo, de Educación

Moravcsik, A. (1998). Europe's integration at century's end. In A. Moravcsik (Ed.), *Centralization or fragmentation? Europe facing the challenges of deepening, diversity, and democracy.* New York: Council on Foreign Relations.

Moreno, L. (2002). Decentralization in Spain. *Regional Studies, 36*(4), 399–408.

Morley, D., & Robins, K. (1995). *Spaces of identity: Global media, electronic landscapes, and cultural boundaries.* London: Routledge.

Morrow, R. A., & Torres, C. A. (2000). The state, globalization, and educational policy. In N. Burbules & C. A. Torres (Eds.), *Globalization and education: Critical perspectives* (pp. 27–56). London: Routledge.

Morrow, R. A., & Torres, C. A. (2003). The state, social movement and educational reform. In R. F. Arnove & C. A. Torres (Eds.), *Comparative education: The dialectic of the global and the local* (pp. 92–114). Oxford, England: Rowman & Littlefield Publishers Inc.

Muñoz, P. M., & Marcos, M. C. (2005). *España: Ayer y hoy* [Spain: Yesterday and today]. New Jersey, NJ: Pearson, Prentice Hill.

Nash, J. C. (2001). *Mayan visions: The quest for autonomy in the age of globalization.* New York: Routledge.

Neal, L., & Barbezat, D. (1998). *The economics of the European Union and the economies of Europe.* New York: Oxford University Press.

Nederveen Pieterse, J. (1995). Globalization as hybridization. In M. Featherstone, S. Lash, & R. Robertson (Eds.), *Global modernities* (pp. 45–68). London: Sage.

Nederveen Pieterse, J. (2004a). *Globalization and culture: Global mélange.* Oxford, England: Rowman & Littlefield Publishers.

Nederveen Pieterse, J. (2004b). *Globalization or empire?* New York: Routledge.

Nóvoa, A. (2002). Ways of thinking about education in Europe. In A. Nóvoa & M. Lawn (Eds.), *Fabricating Europe: The formation of an education space* (pp. 131–156). Dordrecht, Netherlands: Kluwer.

Nóvoa, A., & Lawn, M. (2002). *Fabricating Europe: The formation of an education space.* London: Kluwer Academic Publishers.

Nóvoa, A., & Yariv-Mashal, T. (2003). Comparative research in education: A mode of governance or a historical journey? *Comparative Education, 39*(4), 423–438.

Núñez Seixas, X. M. (2005). From National-Catholic nostalgia to Constitutional patriotism: Conservative Spanish nationalism since the early 1990s. In S. Balfour (Ed.), *The politics of contemporary Spain* (pp. 121–145). New York: Routledge.

Nussbaum, M. (1996). *Patriotism and cosmopolitanism,* 1–6. Retrieved August 26, 2002, from www.phil.uga.edu/faculty/wolf/Nussbaum1.htm

OECD. (1995). *Governance in transition: Public management reforms in OECD countries.* OECD Publishing: Center for Educational Research and Innovation.

OECD. (1996). *The knowledge based economy.* Paris: OECD.

OECD. (1998). *Human capital investment: An international comparison.* OECD Publishing: Center for Educational Research and Innovation.

Offe, C. (1984). *Contradictions of the welfare state.* London: Hutchinson.

Ohmae, K. (1995). *The end of the nation state: the rise of supranational economies.* New York: Free Press.

Ozga, J. (2000). *Policy research in education settings: Contested terrain.* Buckingham, England: Open University Press.

Paqueo, V., & Lammert, J. (2000). *Decentralization & school-based management resource kit.* Washington, DC: World Bank.

Payne, A. (2003). Globalization and modes of supranationalist governance. In D. Held & A. McGrew (Eds.), *The global transformations reader: An introduction to the globalization debate* (pp. 213–222). Cambridge, England: Polity Press.

Peck, J., & Tickell, A. (2002). Neoliberalizing space. *Antipode, 34*(3), 341–624.

Pereyra, M. (2002). Changing educational governance in Spain: Decentralization and control in the autonomous communities. *European Educational Research Journal, 1*(4), 667–675.

Petrongolo, B., & San Segundo, M. J. (2002). Staying-on at school at 16: The impact of labor market conditions in Spain. *Economics of Education Review, 21,* 353–365.

Phillips, D., & Ochs, K. (2003). Processes of policy borrowing in education: Some explanatory and analytical devices. *Comparative Education, 49*(4), 451–461.

Popkewitz, T. (2000). Globalization/supranationalism, knowledge, and the educational practices: Some notes on comparative strategies for educational research. In T. Popkewitz (Ed.), *Educational knowledge: Changing relationships between the state, civil society, and the educational community* (pp. 3–27). Albany, NY: New York Press.

Postlethwaite, N. T. (1999). *International studies of educational achievement: Methodological issues.* Hong Kong: Comparative Educational Research Centre.

Power, M. (1997). *The audit society: Rituals of verification.* Oxford, England: Oxford University Press.

Radaelli, C. (2003). *The open method of coordination-A new governance architecture for the European Union.* Research Report. Swedish Institute for European Policy Studies.

Rizvi, F., Engel, L., Rutkowski, D., & Sparks, J. (2005). *Globalization and recent shifts in educational policy in the Asia Pacific: An overview of some critical issues.* Bangkok, Thailand: UNESCO.

Rizvi, F., & Lingard, B. (2006). Globalization and the changing nature of the OECD's educational work. In H. Lauder, P. Brown, J. Dillabough, & A. H. Halsey (Eds.), *Education, globalization, and social change* (pp. 247–260). Oxford: Oxford University Press.

Robertson, R. (1992). *Globalization: Social theory and global culture.* London: Sage.

Robertson, S. (2007). Embracing the global: Crisis and the creation of a new semiotic order to secure Europe's knowledge-based economy. In N. Fairclough, R. Wodak, & B. Jessop (Eds.), *Education and the knowledge-based economy in Europe.* Netherlands: Sense Publications.

Robertson, S., Bonal, X., & Dale, R. (2002). GATS and the education service industry: The politics of scale and global reterritorialization. *Comparative Education Review, 46*(4), 472–496.

Roller, E. (2004). Conflict and cooperation in EU policy-making: The case of Catalonia. *Perspectives on European Politics and Society, 5*(1), 81–102.

Rondinelli, D. (1990). *Decentralizing urban development programs: A framework for analyzing policy.* Washington, DC: US Agency for International Development.

Rosenau, J. N. (2003). Governance in a new global order. In D. Held & A. McGrew (Eds.), *The global transformations reader: An introduction to the globalization debate* (pp. 223–233). Cambridge, England: Polity Press.

Rubio, R. M. (2000). La Inspección educativa en el estado autonómico [Educational inspection in the State of Autonomies]. In *Congreso National de Inspección Educativa (ACTAS) (150 años de inspección educativa: la inspección ante el siglo XXI)* [National Congress of Educational Inspection (ACTAS) (150 years of educational inspection: Inspection before the 21st century] (pp. 65–82). Madrid, Spain: Grupo Anaya, S.A.

Rutkowski, D. (2007). *Towards a new multilateralism: The development of world education indicators.* Doctoral dissertation, University of Illinois at Urbana-Champaign, USA.

Ryba, R. (1993). La incorporación de la dimension europea al curriculum escolar [Incorporation of the European dimension in school curriculum]. *Revista de Educación* [Journal of Education], *301,* 47–60.

Sabatier, P. A. (1999). The need for better theories. In P. A. Sabatier (Ed.), *Theories of the policy process* (pp. 3–17). Boulder, CO: Westview Press.

Samoff, J. (2003). Institutionalizing international influence. In R. F. Arnove & C. A. Torres (Eds.), *Comparative education: The dialectic of the global and the local* (pp. 409–445). Oxford, England: Rowman & Littlefield Publishers.

Sassen, S. (1996). *Losing control? Sovereignty in the age of globalization.* New York: Columbia UP.

REFERENCES

Sassen, S. (2006). Territory, authority, rights: From medieval to global assemblages. Princeton, NJ: Princeton University Press.

Schäfer, A. (2006). A new form of governance? Comparing the open method of coordination to multilateral surveillance by the IMF and the OECD. *Journal of European Public Policy*, *13*(1), 70–88.

Scholte, J. A. (2000). *Globalization: A critical introduction*. London: Macmillan.

Segura I Mas, A. (2000). Memoria I historia de la transició [Memoir and history of the transition]. In R. Aracil & A. Segura (Eds.), *Memoria de la transició a Espanya i a Catalunya* [Memoir of the transition of Spain and Catalonia]. Barcelona, Spain: University of Barcelona.

Shore, C. (2000). Building Europe: The cultural politics of European integration. London: Routledge.

Smith, N. (2003). Remaking scale: Competition and cooperation in pre-national and post-national Europe. In N. Brenner, B. Jessop, M. Jones, & G. MacLeod (Eds.), *State/Space: A reader* (pp. 227–238). Oxford, England: Blackwell.

Steiner-Khamsi, G. (Ed.). (2004). *The global politics of educational borrowing and lending*. New York: Teachers College Press.

Stone, D. A. (1988). *Policy paradox and political reason*. Illinois, IL: Scott, Foresman and Company.

Stone, D. A. (2002). *Policy paradox: The art of political decision-making* (Rev. ed.). London: W.W. Norton & Company.

Strange, S. (1996). *The retreat of the state: The diffusion of power in the world economy*. Cambridge, England: Cambridge University Press.

Taylor, C. (2002). Modern social imaginaries. *Public Culture*, *14*(1), 91–124.

Taylor, S., Rizvi, F., Lingard, B., & Henry, M. (1997). *Educational policy and the politics of change*. London: Routledge.

Teasley, C. (2004). The culture of discourse on educational reform in Spain. *The Review of Education, Pedagogy, and Cultural Studies*, *26*, 249–275.

Telò, M. (2002). Governance and government in the European Union: The open method of coordination. In M. J. Rodriguez (Ed.), *New knowledge economy in Europe* (pp. 242–271). Cheltenham, England: Edward Elgar.

The Parliament. (2005). *Regions and cities: Local knowledge: Peter Straub, President of the EU's Committee of the Regions talks to Bruno Waterfield*. Retrieved October 3, 2005, from http://www.upolitix.com/EN/News/200510/308d46ac-1c13-41f1-b8f8-3a11588e8171.htm

The Parliament. (2009). *EU's regions to be at the heart of the new 'Lisbon strategy'*. Retrieved May 17, 2009, from http://www.theparliament.com/policy-focus/regions/regions-article/newsarticle/eus-regions-to-be-at-the-heart-of-new-lisbon-strategy/

Tickell, A., & Peck, J. (2003). Making global rules: Globalisation or neoliberalisation. In J. Peck & H. Yeung (Eds.), *Remaking the global economy* (pp. 163–182). London: Sage.

Torres, L., & Piña, V. (2004). Reshaping public administration: The Spanish experience compared to the UK. *Public Administration*, *82*(2), 445–464.

Trubek, D. M., & Trubek, L. G. (2005). Hard and soft law in the construction of social Europe: The role of the open method of co-ordination. *European Law Journal*, *11*(3), 343–364.

Urban, W. J., & Wagoner, J. L. (2003). *American education: A history*. Boston: McGraw Hill.

Villar, G. C. (1984). *Nacional-Catolicismo y escuela: La socialización política del Franquismo* [National-catholicism and the school: The political socialization of Franquismo]. Madrid, Spain: Editorial Hesperia.

Wallerstein, I. (2000). Globalization or the age of transition? A long-term view of the trajectory of the world system. *International sociology*, *15*(2), 249–265.

Williamson, J. (1990). *Latin American adjustment: How much has happened?* Washington, DC: Institute for International Economics.

Wilson, R., & Dissanayake, W. (1996). *Global/local: Cultural production and the transnational imagery*. Durham, NC: Duke University Press.

Wimmer, A. & Glick Shiller, N. (2002). Methodological nationalism and beyond: Nation-state building, migration and the social sciences. *Global Networks*, *2(4)*, 301-334.

World Bank. (2000). *Annual world poverty report.* Washington, DC: World Bank.

World Bank. (2005). Expanding opportunities and building competencies for young people: A new agenda for secondary education. Washington, DC: World Bank.

Wright, S. (2000). Community and communication: The role of language in nation-state building and European integration. Cleveland, OH: Multilingual Matters, LTD.

INDEX

CPSIA information can be obtained at www.ICGtesting.com
Printed in the USA
LVOW070246240812

295745LV00003B/17/P